Microsoft®
OneNote

in One Hour
FOR LAWYERS

BEN M. SCHORR

LawPracticeManagementSection

MARKETING • MANAGEMENT • TECHNOLOGY • FINANCE

Microsoft® is a registered trademark of the Microsoft® Corporation.

Cover design by RIPE Creative, Inc.

Printed in the United States of America

ISBN 978-1-61438-185-3

15 14 13 12   5 4 3 2 1

Library of Congress Cataloging-in-Publication Data

Schorr, Ben M.
    Microsoft OneNote in one hour for lawyers : Ben M. Schorr.
      p. cm.
    Includes bibliographical references and index.
    ISBN 978-1-61438-185-3
    1. Law offices—United States—Automation. 2. Microsoft OneNote. 3. Note-taking—Computer programs. 4. Personal information management—Computer programs. I. Title.
    KF320.A9.S368   2012
    651.7'4028553—dc23

                                                                    2012004909

Discounts are available for books ordered in bulk. Special consideration is given to state bars, CLE programs, and other bar-related organizations. Inquire at Book Publishing, American Bar Association, 321 N. Clark Street, Chicago, Illinois 60654.

www.ShopABA.org

Dedication

To Chris Pratley and Owen Braun who welcomed me down the rabbit hole back when OneNote 2003 was just taking shape.

Table of Contents

About the Author

Ben M. Schorr is a technologist and Chief Executive Officer for Roland Schorr & Tower, a professional consulting firm headquartered in Honolulu, Hawaii with offices in Los Angeles, California and Flagstaff, Arizona. In that capacity he consults with a wide variety of organizations including many law firms. He is frequently sought as a writer, teacher, and speaker for groups as diverse as the Hawaii Visitor and Convention Bureau, Microsoft, and the American Bar Association. More than 16 years ago Microsoft named him as an MVP in their Outlook product group and he has been supporting Outlook, Exchange, Office 365, and most recently OneNote ever since.

Prior to co-founding Roland Schorr, he was the Director of Information Services for Damon Key Leong Kupchak Hastert, a large Honolulu law firm, for almost 8 years.

Mr. Schorr has been a technical editor or contributor on a number of other books over the years. For several years he was half of the "Ask the Exchange Pros" team for Windows Server System magazine. He is the author of *The Lawyer's Guide to Microsoft Outlook 2010* and *The Lawyer's Guide to Microsoft Word 2010*, published by the American Bar Association.

In October of 2005, Mr. Schorr was named by the Pacific Technology Foundation as one of the Top 50 Technology Leaders in Hawaii. He's a member of the Institute of Electrical and Electronics Engineers' (IEEE) Computer Society, the American Bar Association, and the United States Naval Institute.

In his free time Mr. Schorr enjoys coaching football, reading, playing softball, cooking and is a marathoner and Ironman triathlete. He currently lives in Flagstaff, Arizona with his wife Carrie and the cats who keep them around.

You can reach him at bens@rolandschorr.com.

Acknowledgments

I'd like to give some special recognition to the following people:

My parents, Morry and Sharon Schorr, for their constant support, patience, humor and the considerable genetic advantage.

The OneNote MVPs, Kathy Jacobs and Kyoung Soo Jeon.

At Microsoft, Daniel Escapa, Tom Oliver, Alex Simmons, and the rest of the Microsoft OneNote team in Redmond for being terrific and accessible, and giving so much of their time to help me understand how the product works.

My business partner, Matti Raihala, and the rest of the Roland Schorr & Tower team for keeping things running smoothly so I could spend all this time banging out this book.

Tim Johnson, Denise Constantine, Lindsay Dawson, Kimia Shelby, and the LPM Publishing Board. It's one thing to put a bunch of words on pages; another entirely to have it come out the other end as a great looking book. The folks at the ABA take my ramblings and make a book out of them. Bravo.

And, as always, my amaZing wife Carrie who makes every day special.

Introduction

Microsoft OneNote is like tiramisu, a lot of folks have heard of it but not too many know what it really is. The thing is, if attorneys and law firms really got a chance to see it and understand what it can do I think they'd really get excited about it. That's why I'm writing this book. Well, that and they promised me some tiramisu.

Note that this book is *OneNote in One Hour*—and since I only have an hour I'm going to focus on the basics and getting you started. If when you've finished this book you want to know more about OneNote there are a number of resources available for further information and I'll list a few of those in the Resources Appendix at the end.

What Is OneNote?

So what is this thing? Basically it's an electronic replacement for the yellow legal pad—but with a LOT of great features you'll never get on paper. Such as:

- **Full text search**. Take 20 pages of notes and pick out individual words and phrases in moments no matter what page they're on. Try that on paper.
- **Tags**. You can tag your notes with tags that indicate a question, a to-do, an idea or any of a number of other attributes. Taking notes in a meeting? **Lesson 2** is for you and wait until you see what you can do with Question tags that will make you that much more effective in the meeting.
- **Audio recordings**. Don't just take notes on the meeting; record it too (assuming the speaker is ok with that)! Yes, you can do video too. If your audio is good enough OneNote will make it searchable too!

- **Web content.** You can drag and drop content from the web into your notebooks and annotate it too. OneNote will automatically build a hyperlink back to the original site so you can see it in context whenever you like.
- **Screen clippings.** Grab a picture of the entire screen or any little piece of a screen and paste it right into your notebook. Once you've got it in OneNote you can annotate it with text and ink.
- **Insert images.** Take pictures with your digital camera or scanner and insert those right into your notes where you can refer to them, annotate them, or even search them (wait . . . that's coming in a page or two).
- **Drawings.** O.K. you can do that on paper too. But with OneNote you can draw in more than 60 different colors and with different pen thicknesses.
- **Sharing and collaboration.** Share your notes with others inside (or outside) your firm. You can all contribute content, see each other's notes and collaborate in real time.
- **Optical character recognition.** Print PDFs to OneNote or drag in images that have words in them and OneNote will try to recognize the text and make it searchable.
- **Outlook integration.** Send appointments, contacts, tasks or e-mail to OneNote from Outlook and you can take extensive notes on them while preserving the original Outlook items. Create tasks in OneNote and sync them to Outlook so they'll appear on your Outlook tasks list.

What OneNote Isn't

- **A word processor.** One of the complaints I hear about OneNote is that it doesn't have advanced page formatting and layout capabilities and that its printing capabilities are weak. Well . . . that's because it was never intended to produce finished documents. It's a place to capture and organize information and ideas—like a yellow pad. If you decide to create a finished document from that information, that's up to you (but use a different tool for polishing printing).

- **A desktop publisher.** OneNote isn't for doing advanced page layout or printing.
- **A database for highly structured data.** OneNote is for capturing and organizing relatively unstructured data. Thoughts, ideas, research, information. If you want to build an extensive table or database of data you're probably better off with Excel or Access. CAN you do it in OneNote? Yes, but OneNote doesn't have the same kind of tools for managing and organizing structured data as Excel or Access (or even Outlook in some cases).
- **A file archival system.** Yes, you can embed files in OneNote, but it's really not a great place to store large numbers of files just for the sake of storing files.
- **An e-mail archival system.** Yes, you can send e-mail to OneNote, but it's not a great choice as a repository of massive quantities of e-mail messages.

What Do You Need to Have to Use OneNote?

You need a computer, of course, running Windows XP Service Pack 3 or later. It doesn't have to be a Tablet PC, though OneNote really shines on a Tablet PC with its inking capabilities. I use OneNote on desktop and laptops all the time—I just have to type my notes rather than inking them. If you've ever seen my handwriting you'd know that's probably not a bad idea anyhow.

Worth mentioning that if you really want ink capabilities on a desktop (or laptop) you can buy after-market tablets like the Wacom Bamboo that will let you use the pen in OneNote. I have one on my desktop machine and it works fairly well for those occasions when I want to pull out the pen and sketch a bit.

What . . . No Mac Version?

Nope. The Mac is a significantly different operating system and, especially as there is no Mac Tablet PC (the iPad doesn't count—that's iOS not OS X), the decision was made not to expend the resources to support a platform that has such small market share AND for which relatively easy workarounds exist. If you have a Mac and want to run OneNote you have a couple of options:

1. Install VMWare Fusion or Parallels and run the Windows version of OneNote in a VM.
2. Use the web-based version of OneNote which is free on Office Live.

So How Do I Get OneNote?

Well, if you have Microsoft Office 2010 then you probably already have OneNote 2010 installed on your computer. Just click the **Start** button, go to Programs (or "All Programs" depending upon your version of Windows) find the Microsoft Office group and it should be right there—like it is for me in **Figure 1**.

Figure 1

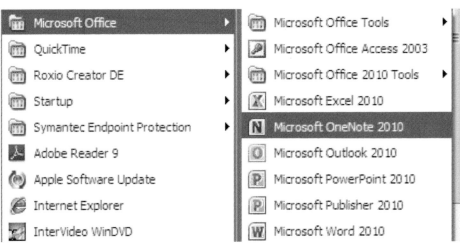

If you have Office 2007 then it depends upon which version of Office 2007 you have. If you have the Home & Student or Ultimate versions then you have OneNote 2007. If you don't . . . well, you don't.

OneNote can be purchased separately from all fine software retailers, including **Amazon.com** and even directly from Microsoft.

Getting Started

So, let's get started with OneNote. OneNote uses the metaphor of a spiral bound notebook. You have a notebook and within that notebook you have sections. Within each section you have pages. Simple as that. How you choose to organize your notebooks is up to you. **Figure 2** shows you how OneNote looks when you've got a brand new notebook open.

Figure 2

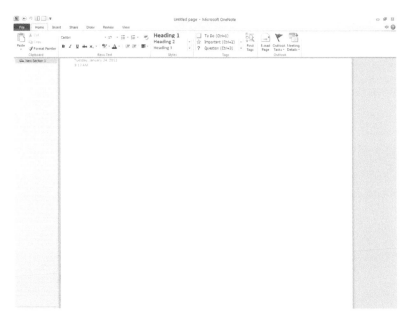

When you first launch OneNote 2010 it will ask you where you want to locate your first notebook—on the web or on your local computer. I recommend putting it on your local computer—it's just an easier way to get started. You can always create a web-hosted notebook later if you like.

Once you get OneNote started you'll find that it has one or two sample notebooks already created. Those have some useful information and demonstrations of things you can do with OneNote, so they're worth browsing through.

The Ribbon

Across the top of the OneNote screen you'll find the now-familiar Ribbon (see **Figure 3**). At the very top, on the title bar, you'll see the Quick Access Toolbar or QAT and just below that a row of tabs that give you access to pretty much every function in the product. We'll talk more about some of those functions in the lessons to come.

Figure 3

You can minimize the Ribbon, as I often do, by pressing **CTRL+F1** on your keyboard or by clicking the little "up arrow" on the right-end of the Ribbon next to the **Help** button (see **Figure 4**). To re-maximize the Ribbon just press **CTRL+F1** again or click the **Minimize** button again.

Figure 4

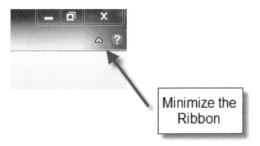

Minimize the Ribbon

The Quick Access Toolbar (QAT)

As I mentioned previously, the QAT is located at the very top (by default; you can move it if you want to) on the title bar of OneNote. It contains a few icons by default—things like "Back" and shortcuts for various Outlook views like "Docked View" or "Full Screen." You can add any OneNote command you like to it though and that's a handy way to get . . . well . . . quick access (hence the name) to those commands. To show you how to do that let's add a command that was curiously left off the Ribbon: Undo.

1. Click the drop arrow on the right-end of the QAT.
2. Select **Undo** from the list that appears.

Figure 5 shows you what that's going to look like.

Figure 5

O.K., that was a little too easy. Let's try adding something that ISN'T on the frequently used commands list.

1. Click the drop arrow on the right-end of the QAT.
2. Click **More Commands**
3. Above the list on the left, under "Choose commands from" select **All commands**
4. Scroll down to **Move or Copy** and select it.
5. Click the **Add** button in the middle of the dialog box to add it to the list on the right.
6. Use the arrow keys on the far right side to move it up to just below "Full Page View."
7. Click **OK** to exit.

Figure 6 gives you an idea of how that process will look.

Figure 6

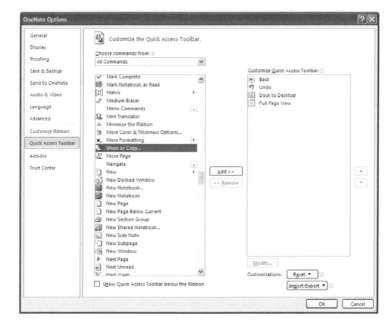

Now you can see your new **Move or Copy** button right where you placed it on the QAT (see **Figure 7**). This is especially handy when you want to file (or re-file) notes in different sections or notebooks.

Figure 7

Your new "Move or Copy" button.

Navigation Pane

Along the left side of the screen in OneNote is the Navigation Pane. This contains the list of notebooks and sections that you currently have open in OneNote (see **Figure 8**). The larger headings that you see are

Figure 8

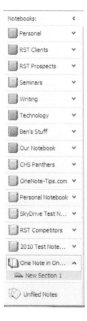

the notebooks and within those notebooks you can see the sections (and section groups; we'll get to those in a bit).

The red and green icons you may see next to the notebook names indicate the synchronization status of notebooks that are saved somewhere other than the local hard drive. We'll talk more about synchronization (and where to save notebooks) shortly. If you don't see a red or green icon that just means the notebook isn't shared it's just stored on your local hard drive.

To expand a notebook just click the downward arrow you see on the right-end of the notebook name.

So let's get started with creating a notebook in OneNote.

Notebooks

Creating a new Notebook in OneNote 2010 is a fairly simple process with one somewhat important decision to make. Click **File** (on the Ribbon, at the top of the screen) to get to the Backstage area and then click **New** to create your new notebook. You'll get a screen that looks similar to **Figure 9**.

The first question it's asking you is the big decision you have to make: Where do you want to store this notebook? You have three basic choices:

Web

If you select Web, OneNote will store your new notebook on SkyDrive under your **Live.com** account. **Live.com** is a free Microsoft service which competes with Google's online offerings. When you sign up for **Live.com** (did I mention it's free?) you get an e-mail address (what used to be called "Hotmail"), Instant Messenger, space for a blog and

Figure 9

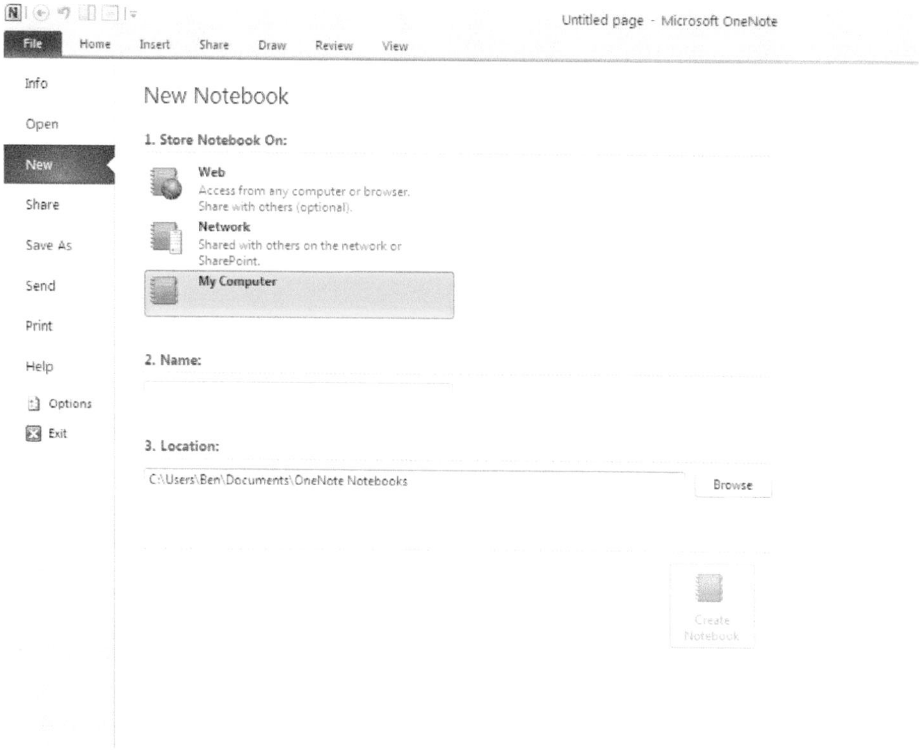

25GB of storage space, called "SkyDrive," for whatever kind of files you want.

OneNote 2010 is SkyDrive aware so you can store your notebooks there if you want to.

What About Dropbox?

You might be tempted to store your OneNote notebooks on Dropbox or some other 3rd party sync service. Resist. Those services aren't

OneNote-aware and OneNote doesn't know about them either. OneNote has a somewhat complex background sync going on all of the time—even when you have the notebooks stored on your local hard drive. If you use a 3rd party sync service like Dropbox it's POSSIBLE that Dropbox will accidentally overwrite your OneNote file with what it thinks is the latest version, meanwhile OneNote has a more recent version in cache. The result? Potentially lost data or file corruption. Just use SkyDrive if you want to store your notebooks in the cloud or sync them across the Internet. It's not worth risking corrupted or lost data.

Why Would You Want To?

If you're going to share your notebooks between multiple machines or multiple users and they won't always be on the same local network SkyDrive is a good option.

If you're going to occasionally want to use the OneNote Web app (see **Lesson 4**) then SkyDrive is a good choice.

If you're going to use the OneNote for iPhone app then you'll have to store your notebook on SkyDrive if you want to synchronize it to the iPhone. The iPhone app requires SkyDrive.

Why Wouldn't You Want To?

If the notebook contains especially sensitive information then you might be justifiably wary of storing it in "the cloud" of SkyDrive. SkyDrive is reasonably secure for most common uses, but it's not HIPAA compliant or heavily encrypted. You should think carefully about storing confidential client data in ANY cloud-based storage location.

Network

The second storage option you have is to store your new notebook on your network or on a SharePoint server. This will usually apply to business users who may have a network server (or several) to store files, though increasingly we're seeing home users who have a shared drive somewhere in their network that multiple machines can access.

Why Would You Want To?

You might choose this option if you want to share the notebook among multiple users or machines that are all part of the same law firm or office (and thus have at least occasional access to the server location where you're going to store the notebook) and you don't want to let this data outside of the office firewall. This is a popular choice for how to store/share sensitive client data.

My wife and I have a network attached storage device at home and I've used this option to store a notebook that we share for our household information. She doesn't have a **Live.com** account (and wasn't interested in having one) so it was easier to just share it on our home network.

Why Wouldn't You Want To?

If you're not going to share this notebook with any other devices, or if you need to share this notebook with people who don't have access to your company server.

If you're going to sync this notebook to your iPhone you'll have to put the notebook on SkyDrive, you can't currently access network drives or SharePoint sites from the iPhone version of OneNote.

My Computer

The simplest option of all—this will store the OneNote notebook on your local computer. The default location on "My Computer" is in the "OneNote Notebooks" folder of your "My Documents" folder as you can see in **Figure 10**.

Figure 10

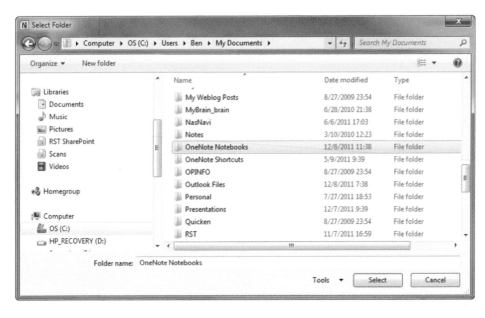

Why Would You Want To?

The simplest choice—you don't need any network connectivity at all to locate a notebook on your local drive. These notebooks are the most private and secure—nobody can access these files unless they have access to your local hard drive.

Why Wouldn't You Want To?

It's much harder to share notebooks that are located on your local drive either with other people or between multiple devices of your own.

Sections

Once you've created your notebook you'll need to create your first section. Every notebook has to have at least one section. You almost can't avoid creating that section—clicking anywhere on the note page will create that first section. In **Figure 11** you'll see the tabs across the top that represent your sections.

Figure 11

To create additional sections you can either click on the tab on the far right-end of the section tabs or right-click on any section (either on the tabs or on the navigation pane at the left) and select "New Section."

What's a Section Group?

A section group is just an organizational construct that lets you group multiple sections together. Almost like having a section and sub-sections. In practice I rarely use them and rarely encourage them; they mostly just seem to add a layer of confusion and obfuscation.

Give your section a name . . . then it's time to start creating pages.

Pages

The page is the basic unit of OneNote. Ultimately all of your notes will be on a collection of pages—organized into sections, within notebooks. **Figure 12** shows a new, blank, page.

You can create as many pages as you like and you can create sub-pages of your pages if you want to.

The page is like a limitless sheet of paper that just goes on and on . . . not just vertically but horizontally as well if you want it to. I generally keep the horizontal spread to a minimum on my pages. It's just less intuitive to scroll left and right as opposed to up and down. So I tend to add content vertically for the most part.

Figure 12

At the top of your page is the Page Title field. If you don't type anything here OneNote will just use whatever you type closest to the top of the page as the title. I encourage you to give your pages a decent title, though. It makes organization easier and cleaner.

You can always change the page title later if you like.

Click anywhere on the page and you can start typing notes or drawing with the pens. In the next lesson we'll get into the details of how to take notes. For now just know that you can click and type—simple as that.

Later we'll also talk about reorganizing your notebooks or sections and moving (or copying) pages from place to place.

To create a new page just click the **New Page** button at the top of the page list on the right.

Page Colors

There are 16 very subtle colors you can choose for your pages—well, 17 if you count "White"—and to make that choice just go to the View tab of the Ribbon and click **Page Colors** to see the gallery you see in **Figure 13**. The colors are awfully subtle on all but the brightest screens and I rarely bother with them myself.

Figure 13

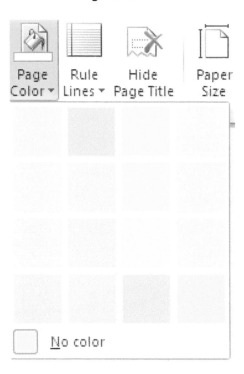

If you select a page color and decide later that you don't like it you can always change it without affecting the page content later.

Rule Lines

OneNote includes some page formats that include rule lines—those horizontal lines we all learned to write on when we had notebook paper. And writing on the lines is why they're in OneNote too—if you're inking on your note pages the rule lines help keep your writing straight.

You can choose from a variety of line styles. Just go to the View tab on the Ribbon and choose **Rule Lines** to get the gallery. There you can select from a variety of line widths or you can even select line types that are grids, like you see in **Figure 14**.

Figure 14

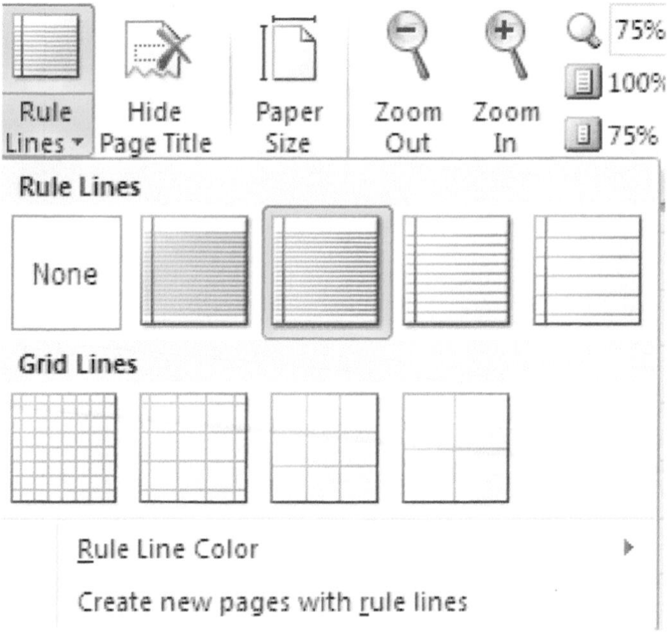

The lines don't serve any function if you're typing your notes, in fact it's rather hard to get your typed notes to align on the lines anyhow. I usually just turn them off which you can do pretty easily on the View tab by clicking the **Rule Lines** button.

Like page colors you can always turn the lines off later if you want to—it won't affect the notes you've taken on the page.

What About Printing the Lines?

If you're using an older version of OneNote (2003 or 2007) you may have noticed that the rule lines don't print. There is a workaround for that. Create a blank page with rule lines, use the screen clipping feature (**Windows Key + S**) and screen grab the rule lines. Turn the rule lines off on the page and paste the lines you just captured. Right-click that image and set it to be in the background. Now you can take your notes right over the top of that and when you print the lines will print.

OneNote 2010 eliminates the need for that workaround—the lines can print in OneNote 2010.

Subpages

For organizational purposes you can create subpages of your pages. Do they function differently than pages? No. They're just indented. In fact, in a OneNote 2010 notebook you can have TWO levels of subpages— just in case you're craving a sub-subpage.

To create a subpage click the down-arrow on the **New Page** button at the top right (see **Figure 15**) and choose **New Subpage**. Or you can just

Figure 15

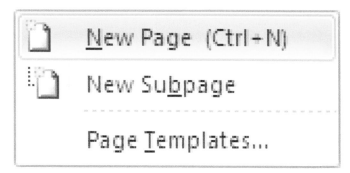

create a new regular page and then drag it to the right with your mouse. Or you can right-click a page and choose **Make Subpage.** ➡ Make Subpage There are a bunch of ways to make a subpage.

Saving

One of the things about OneNote that sometimes stymies newcomers is that there isn't any obvious way to save your notes. That's because OneNote saves your notes automatically, in the background, every few seconds. If you really want to you can press **CTRL+S** to save, but there's no point.

OneNote DOES have a Save As function, you can find that under the File tab (what we call "Backstage") on the Ribbon (see **Figure 16**).

Figure 16

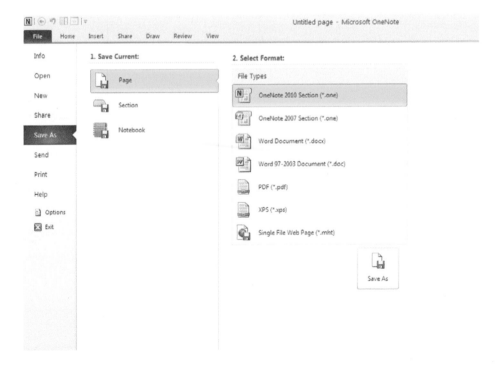

You would use that if you want to save a copy of the current section as a new OneNote file or perhaps if you wanted to save it as Word document or PDF to share with somebody else.

Cache File

No matter where you choose to save your notebooks—on SkyDrive, on your network or on your local computer—OneNote actually does all of its work on a local cache file. Then in the background the changes to that cache file are synchronized to the main notebook file. There are several reasons for that—including performance and reliability. Where you'll really appreciate it is if you're using OneNote on a portable computer and you go to open your notebooks when you're on the road and don't have direct access to them—maybe they're on your office network or SkyDrive and you're disconnected. What you'll find is that you have your entire notebook right there like always. You can read them, make any changes you like and the next time you're connected to the location where the notebook is shared (and OneNote is open) OneNote will automatically sync the changes to the notebook for you.

Taking Notes

OneNote is all about taking notes—that's its primary function. It puts a lot of tools in your hands to make your notes more effective and to let you choose what kind of notes you want to take.

Standard Text

The most obvious example of note taking is just typing text on a page. To start taking notes just click anywhere on a page and start typing. Yes, it really is just that easy (see **Figure 17**).

Figure 17

New Section 1

Good Guys v Bad Guys
Tuesday, January 24, 2012
9:37 AM

Let's take some notes...

OneNote even lets you do something else that isn't very easy to do with your yellow legal pad—rearrange your notes and insert space in the middle for additional notes.

To move your notes on the page just grab the note handle ⊞ and drag/drop the notes to wherever you like with your mouse. You can also right-click the note and choose "Move" then use the arrow keys on your keyboard to move the note container wherever you like (see Figure 18).

Figure 18

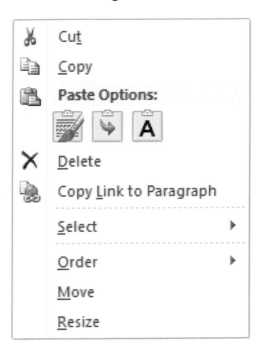

If you want to move your note to another page you can do that, but you'll need to cut/paste the notes by selecting them with your mouse, pressing **CTRL+X** (or right-click and choose "Cut" or click the **Cut** button on the Ribbon) then navigating to the place you want to place those notes, clicking there on the page and pressing **CTRL+V** (or click the **Paste** button on the Ribbon).

If you'd like to insert space between your notes, click the **Insert Space** button on the Insert tab of the Ribbon ≝ , then move your mouse to where you want to insert the space, hold down the left mouse button and drag down to insert the space you need as you see in **Figure 19**.

Figure 19

You can also use the Insert Space tool to remove space. If you find you've got a lot of white space between the bottom of a note and the top of the next note just launch the Insert Space tool from the Ribbon, go to the top of the note you'd like to move up, hold the left mouse button and drag UP to remove that excess white space.

You can type your notes in sentences, bullet points, or just random words if you like. You can do some limited formatting of your notes, which is to say that you can select the font, font color, font size, etc. that you want the text to be in. You can also apply highlighting, numbered or bulleted lists and even tables (hold on, we'll get there in a minute). The tools you see in the Basic Text group of the Ribbon (see **Figure 20**) should be familiar to you from other Office products and can help you make your notes look the way you want them to.

Figure 20

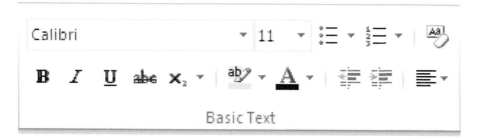

I rarely change the typeface of my notes, but I DO occasionally use different colored text and boldface to make different text elements stand out.

To apply bullet points to your notes you can just preface the first bullet point with an asterisk ("*") and then press space before typing your notes. OneNote will automatically convert the * to a bullet and for each additional point as you press Enter to start your next point OneNote will automatically create another bulleted item as you can see in **Figure 21**.

Figure 21

- These notes have bullets.
- This one.
- And this one, too!

To stop applying bullets press Enter to start a new line then press Backspace to delete the bullet and you can continue from there.

To apply bullets to an existing list just select the list with your mouse and click the **Bullets** button ≔ ▾ on the Ribbon or press the CTRL+ hotkey.

If you have a stylus or tablet you can take your notes in ink rather than typing them. OneNote will even try to recognize and index what you write so that it can be searched. A couple of things that are important to know about OneNote's handwriting recognition:

- It can't be trained. It just is what it is and you can't make it better.
- You can't scan in handwritten notes or notes written on some other machine and have OneNote recognize the text. The recognition works by watching your pen strokes on the screen, if it doesn't see you write the notes it's not going to be able to figure out what you wrote.

Tags

Tags are little flags that you can assign to paragraphs of note text in order to categorize them. OneNote comes with a list of predefined tags or you can create/customize your own.

To use one of the predefined tags place the cursor in front of the text you want to tag, then look to the Tags gallery on the Home tab of the Ribbon. Select the tag you like and it will be applied to your text. You can apply as many tags as you like to a piece of text; though obviously at some point it gets ridiculous if you have 11 tags applied to the same sentence. **Figure 22** shows you the tags gallery and some of your choices.

Figure 22

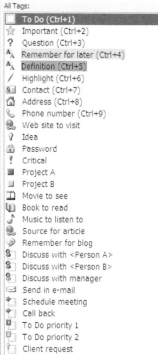

Some of the tags are interactive—for example you can apply the checkbox tab to your text, then when that particular item is complete you can click the checkbox to apply a check in the box. **Figure 23** shows before and after of the checkbox tags.

Figure 23

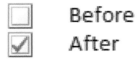

To create your own tags expand the Tags gallery and click "Customize Tags." From there you can create a new tag or modify an existing one. Give your tag an icon, a name and, optionally, a hotkey sequence that will let you apply it from the keyboard. **Figure 24** shows the New Tag dialog box.

Figure 24

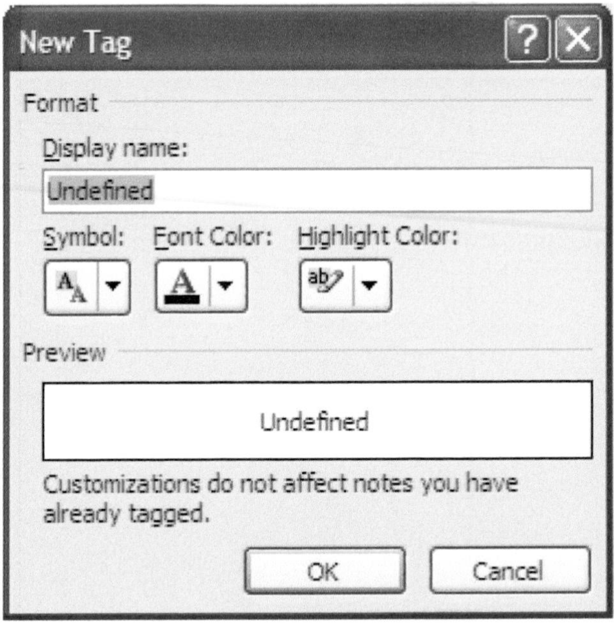

Later in this lesson we're going to talk about how you can search for your tags. This is especially useful in meetings when you need to aggregate your questions or produce a quick report to see what action items everybody has.

If you want to use a custom tag to aggregate or easily find content you don't have to create a formal tag per se. You can always just use a unique text string in your notes and then search for that text string. For example: #ActGregB# could be a tag to indicate an action item for Greg Barnes.

In **Lesson 5** we're going to talk about some special flags you can assign to your notes in order to have those notes appear as To-Do items in Outlook.

Tables

OneNote lets you organize your notes into tables if you like. The tables are fairly primitive—you can't do calculations on them the way you can with Excel, but they're easy and a nice organizational context for some kinds of content.

To create a table just type the text you want in the first cell, then just press the TAB key. OneNote will create the second column cell for you and you can just type. Press TAB again to create another column or press Enter to go to the next row. **Figure 25** shows you a table.

Figure 25

Feature	Supported?
Columns	Yes
Calculations	No
Nested Tables	Yes
iPhone App Support	Not Yet

To add a new column or row just right click the table where you'd like to add the column or row, choose Table from the context menu and then Insert Left/Right/Above/Below as appropriate. A new row or column will be inserted for you (see **Figure 26**).

Figure 26

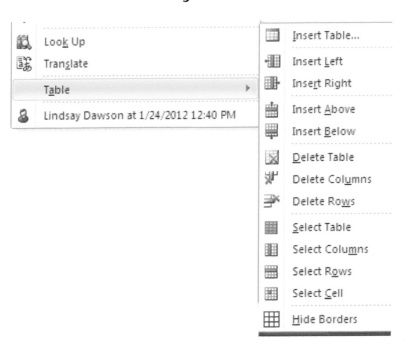

One thing to keep in mind about tables is that if you're going to access these notes with the iPhone app that tables are not currently (as of this writing) supported on the iPhone app. So any notes you put in tables . . . won't be viewable there.

Styles

OneNote 2010 gives you a primitive set of Styles that you can use in formatting your notes (see **Figure 27**). Much like Word, styles are pre-defined sets of formatting that you can apply to standardize your for-

Figure 27

matting a bit. I rarely use them myself—again OneNote really isn't intended for creating finished documents. To apply styles just select the style you want from the Styles gallery on the Home tab of the Ribbon.

Unlike Word you can't customize OneNote's styles at all. I'd probably use them more often if I could create my own custom styles for common formatting elements.

Draw/Shapes/Ink

Drawing in OneNote is best done with a stylus or tablet. If you don't have one available you can still get the job done with the mouse.

OneNote makes some shapes available for you and also you can free-hand draw with the available "pens." To do a little drawing in OneNote go to the Draw tab on the Ribbon as you see in **Figure 28**. There you can select a pen to write with or select one of the pre-designed shapes to insert.

Figure 28

To use a pen, just click it in the "Tools" group of the Draw tab then move your stylus or mouse down to the page and start drawing away!

If you want to customize your pen click the dropdown at the bottom right corner of the pens gallery (see **Figure 29**) to drop down the extended gallery you see in **Figure 30** and choose "More color and thickness options" to get the Pen Properties dialog you see in **Figure 31**. There you can select from dozens of different colors and 9 different pen thicknesses. Once you've made your selection that pen will be added to the standard pens gallery so you can easily reuse it anytime you want.

To use a shape select the shape from the Insert Shapes group (and yes, I know there are only about 11 shapes provided), then click the **Color & Thickness** button to open the Color and Thickness dialog box

Figure 29

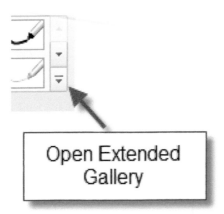

Open Extended Gallery

Figure 30

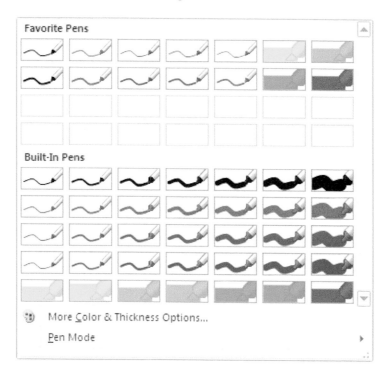

Figure 31

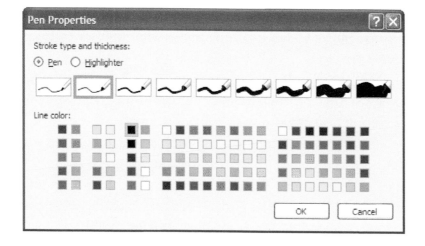

you see in **Figure 32**. Looks a lot like the Pen Properties dialog box, doesn't it? Select a color and line thickness for your shape, then move your mouse to where you want it on the page, hold down the left mouse button and drag the mouse out to create the shape. You can always adjust/resize it later so don't worry if it's not perfect the first time.

Figure 32

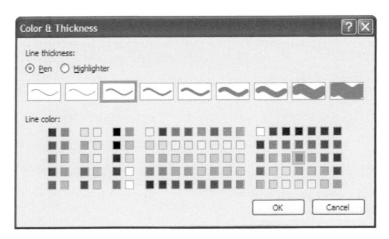

If you draw something you'd like to remove OneNote provides a handy eraser tool. Towards the left end of the Ribbon you'll find the **Eraser** button and pay attention to the drop-down arrow at the bottom of the button. That lets you specify what kind of eraser it is (see **Figure 33**).

- The Small/Medium/Large eraser settings are just what you'd think they are. Different thicknesses of "eraser head" depending upon how broad a swath you wish to cut through your ink.
- The Stroke eraser is actually a very clever way to erase an entire ink stroke in a single click. Great for when you just make ONE line out of place and don't want to have to try and surgically extract that line with the smallest possible eraser . . . all the while careful not to accidentally nick any of your other, more perfect, lines.

Figure 33

A Few things you should know about the ink:

1. They can't really be anchored to the page. Though recent updates to OneNote 2010 have made them more predictable, they do have a tendency to move around—especially if you add things above them.
2. They can't really be anchored to each other. When they move they won't always move the same distance. OneNote 2010 doesn't provide a way to group ink items together. That can occasionally be a problem if you have multiple ink objects that point at or relate to each other. You should spot check them to make sure they haven't changed positions before sharing/printing your notes.
3. Neither the OneNote web app nor the iPhone app currently support displaying ink.

One place that ink is frequently used in OneNote is to annotate images, notes, printouts or clippings (see **Figure 34**).

Figure 34

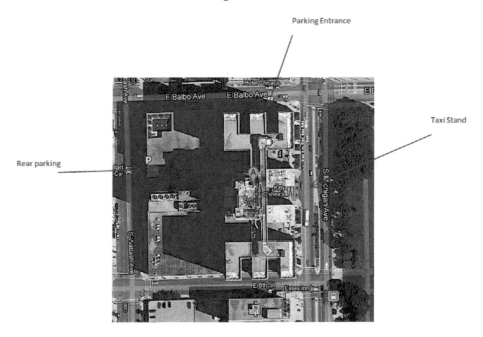

Click the **Select & Type** button on the left end of the Ribbon (in the Draw tab) to get back to the normal cursor.

Audio

If you want to record audio in your notes all you need is a microphone. If you have a laptop you probably have a built-in microphone and that might be sufficient—though for good audio you'll probably want a better external microphone. A number of good microphones are available and aren't especially pricey.

On the Insert tab you'll see the **Record Audio** button but beware . . . when you click it OneNote will start recording right away. When you start recording the "Audio & Video" tab will appear on the Ribbon and there you do have controls to pause or stop the recording, as you can see in **Figure 35**.

Figure 35

BONUS: If your audio is clear enough OneNote will try to do voice recognition on it and index the words. That means you can do a full text search of your audio recordings too. That's what we call in the business: Super Cool.

When you go to play your audio notes back OneNote will do a "Follow the bouncing ball" thing where it highlights the notes you were taking while that audio was being recorded (see **Figure 36**). One limitation—the notes have to be on the same page with the recording.

Figure 36

This is text I'm taking notes on.

Another reason to get an external microphone, other than sound quality, is that the built-in microphones on most laptops will tend to pick up the clickity-clack of the keyboard as you type notes and that sound can sometimes drown out (or at least obscure) what you're trying to record.

You can insert audio files recorded elsewhere into your notes, for example if you recorded them with your portable digital recorder or with a smartphone, but OneNote won't do the "follow along" trick unless you recorded the notes in OneNote to begin with.

Video

Next to Record Audio on the Insert tab is Record Video  . If you have an attached camera you can record video just the same way you record audio.

The video recordings are in .WMV or .AVI format and can be easily shared even with people who don't have OneNote.

OneNote will, unless you have the option turned off, automatically try to search the audio track of your video recordings for words just as it does with audio files.

To record video just click the **Record Video** button on the Ribbon. Be forewarned, just like the audio, as soon as you click that button it will start recording.

If you want to delete either an audio or video recording from your notes you have to select it with your mouse and press the Delete key. You'll probably also need to select and delete the "Video recording started . . ." text that OneNote automatically inserts too (see **Figure 37**).

Figure 37

Audio recording started: 3:31 PM Tuesday, January 24, 2012

Side Notes

One of the most powerful tools in OneNote is the ability to just quickly capture random notes. Those notes that used to end up on Post-its on your monitor or scraps of paper on your desk . . . OneNote gives you a better way to capture and organize them. **Figure 38** shows you a side note in action.

To start a Side Note just press **Windows Key + N** on your keyboard. A small note will open on the screen and you can type any thoughts or notes you want. I often find myself with a half a dozen of

Figure 38

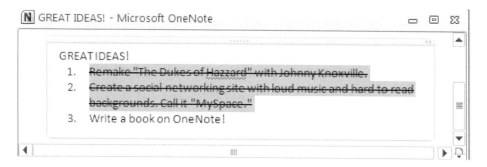

these little note windows scattered around my screen as I capture random ideas. If you close the note it will be saved in the "Unfiled Notes" notebook of OneNote until you move it somewhere else (see **Figure 39**).

Figure 39

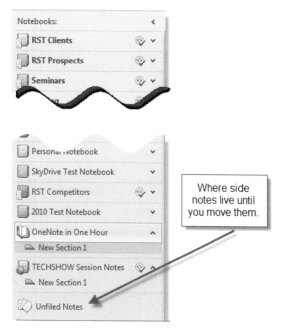

OneNote's little side note secret? Side notes are just regular note pages in a small window set to "Full Page View." If you click the button on the Quick Access Toolbar (QAT) to turn off **Full Page View** the entire OneNote interface will appear.

Yes, the opposite works too—if you are working in a regular OneNote window and click the button for **Full Page View** you'll switch into what looks like a really big side note.

Keep on Top

Occasionally when I'm taking notes on something I want to keep my notes on top of other windows so that I can refer to them or quickly access them to type more. In **Figure 40** you'll notice a **push-pin** button on the View tab of the Ribbon. If you click that OneNote will keep your side note window on top of any other windows you have open. Even when OneNote doesn't have focus (which means you're actually using some other application) the side note window will stay visible on top.

Figure 40

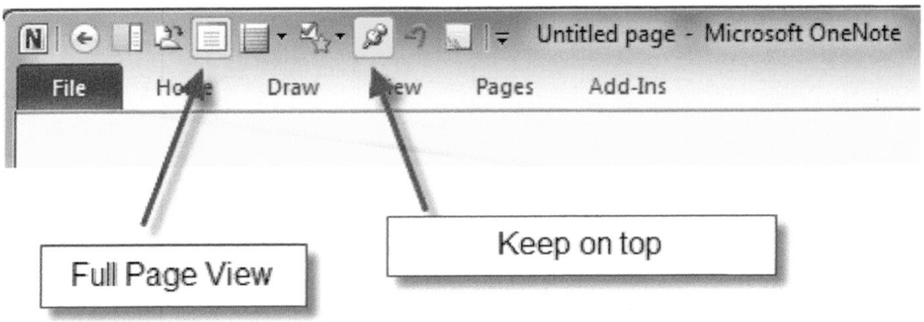

Previous Page/Next Page

Side Notes are kept in a custom notebook called "Unfiled Notes." You can move them, of course, but by default when you create a new Side Note you're creating a page in the Unfiled Notes notebook. Going to the Pages tab and clicking **Next Page** or **Previous Page** (see **Figure 41**) lets you cycle through the other notes in Unfiled Notes—handy if you want to access the side note you created 10 minutes ago, for instance.

Figure 41

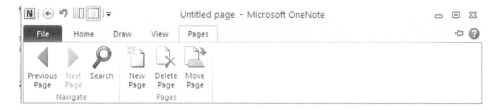

File Those Notes

If you want to file that new side note in a notebook or section you've already got just click the **Move Page** button to get the "Move or Copy Pages" dialog you see in **Figure 42**. From there you can select any notebook or section and the page will be moved (or copied, if you really want) to that location.

Figure 42

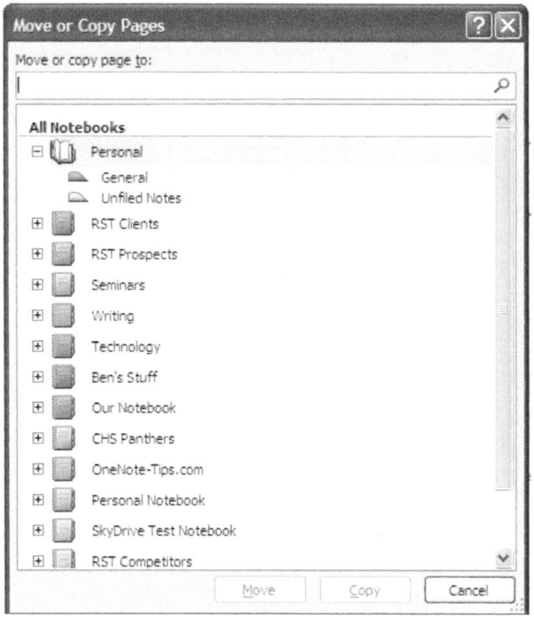

Multiple Windows

Want two OneNote pages side by side? Go to the View tab and click the **New Window** button   . You can open as many different OneNote pages at a time as you like (but be careful, each new window you open consumes system resources and they're finite). It's not unusual for me to have two regular OneNote pages open at a time and maybe 3 or 4 side notes open too.

Hyperlinks

One of the powerful capabilities of OneNote is the ability to link notes to each other and to outside content. There are several ways to create a hyperlink in OneNote.

Wikilinks

When you're typing your notes if you know that you want a particular word (or phrase) to link to a page with that word (or phrase) as the title you can simply enclose the word (or phrase) in double-brackets, like this: "The construction expert on this case is [[Justin Steffey]]." When you press space the double-brackets will disappear and the enclosed text will be turned into a hyperlink.

If a page with that title already exists the hyperlink will automatically be built to that page. If the page doesn't exist then the hyperlink will have a broken blue line like in **Figure 43**. Click on that hyperlink and you'll be taken to a clean new page with that text as the title. Once you've created the page the blue line will turn solid like a traditional hyperlink.

Figure 43

Justin Steffey

Links to OneNote Content

You can create links to any paragraph, page, section or notebook in OneNote. To create a hyperlink to an existing piece of OneNote content simply right-click on that piece of content and choose "Copy link to [Paragraph/Page/Section/Notebook]" (see **Figure 44**). Then go to the text you want to link from, select it, right-click and choose **Link** (or press **CTRL+K**) (see **Figure 45**).

Figure 44

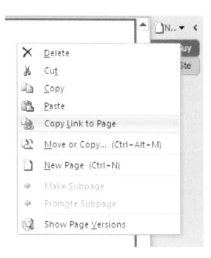

Figure 45

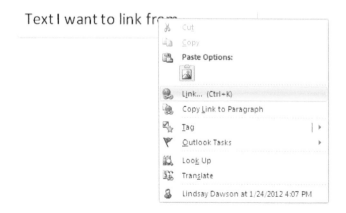

Right-click in the address field and choose **Paste** (or press **CTRL+V**) to paste the link address into that field as you can see in **Figure 46**. Click **OK** and your link is created!

Figure 46

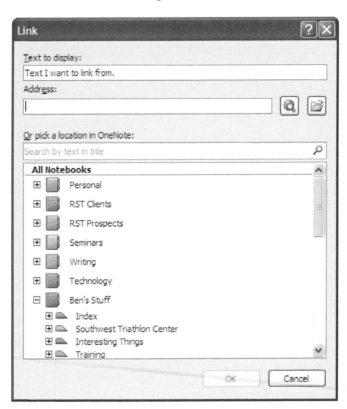

Links to Outside Content

If you want to create a hyperlink to something outside of OneNote, like a webpage, just select that address with your mouse, press **CTRL+C** to copy that address to the clipboard, then highlight the text in OneNote that you want to be the hyperlink, press **CTRL+K** and paste the address into the address field (see **Figure 47**).

Figure 47

Templates

If you're going to use OneNote to create a more structured notebook you may want to use some templates to help guide your note taking.

OneNote comes with a surprisingly large set of templates, but it's also possible to create and use your own.

Built in Templates

If you click the drown arrow to the right-end of the **New Page** button above the page list you'll get a menu with a lot of options for creating a new page (see **Figure 48**). At the bottom of that menu is "Page Tem-

Figure 48

plates. . . ." Select that and you'll get the Templates task pane like you see in **Figure 49**. Here you'll find a few different categories of template such as Academic, Business, Decorative, Planners and the imaginatively named "Blank."

Figure 49

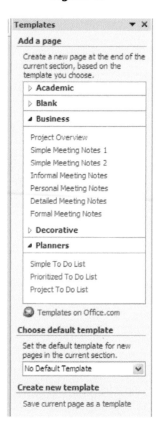

These built-in templates were created by Microsoft's designers and they feature some ideas to get you started on a particular kind of notes. Meeting notes, lecture notes, to do lists and more.

Creating Custom Templates

If none of the built-in templates excite you then you can easily create your own. How? Just set up a page exactly the way you want your template to look, go into the Templates task pane (see **Figure 49** previously) and at the bottom of the templates task pane you'll see a link for "Save current page as a template." Click that, OneNote will ask you to name your new template and give you the option to make it the default template for the current section (see **Figure 50**).

Figure 50

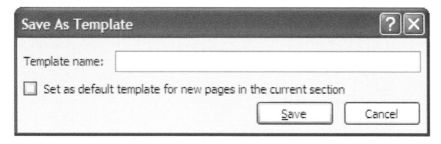

Let's try one . . .

1. Start from a blank page.
2. Click the View tab of the Ribbon and set the Page Color to yellow (see **Figure 51**).
3. Click the **Rule Lines** button and select one of the middle options (see **Figure 52**).
4. Click the **Paper Size** button and set the paper size to "Legal" (see **Figure 53**).

Figure 51

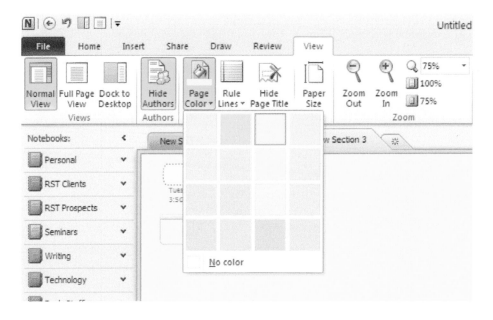

Figure 52

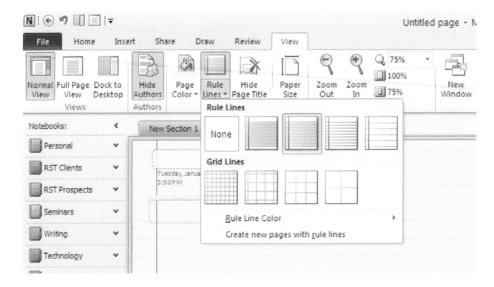

Figure 53

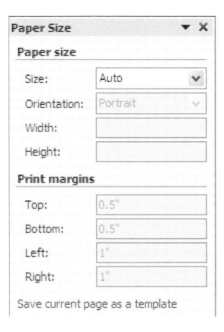

5. Click the drop down next to New Page and select "Page Templates . . ." (as we did in **Figure 48** previously).
6. Click "Save current page as a template" (as we did in **Figure 49** previously).
7. Name the template "Yellow Legal Pad" and check the box to make it the default for the current section (see **Figure 54**).

Figure 54

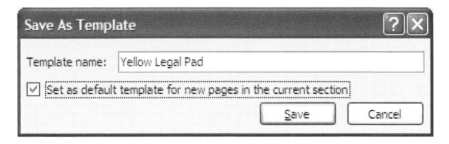

Great! Now create a new page in your section. Voila . . . a yellow legal pad just like **Figure 55**.

Figure 55

If you want to change the default template for the section back to the regular, blank, page go back into the Templates task pane and just above the "Save current page as a template" link you'll find a selection box that lets you choose which template you want to use as the default. "Default—Blank" should reset you to the original condition.

If you want to add other elements to your templates feel free. One thing you might want to add is a graphical element. The easiest way is to use the screen clipping tool (we'll talk about that in **Lesson 3**) to grab your drawing, image or picture and paste it wherever on the page you want it. If you want the image to be part of the background (so you can easily type over the top of it and it won't move) then there is a bit of a trick to it. If you just paste a clipped image onto your page OneNote won't let you set it as a background. What you need to do is drag the pasted clipping out of the note container that it's in. Alternatively you could insert an image via the **Picture** button on the Insert tab or by copying and pasting (the traditional way) the image into your notes. Then right-click that image (or images) and select "Set Image as Background" as you can see in **Figure 56**. Be judicious with this though—the more images and graphics you insert on the page the more storage space the notebook will require.

Figure 56

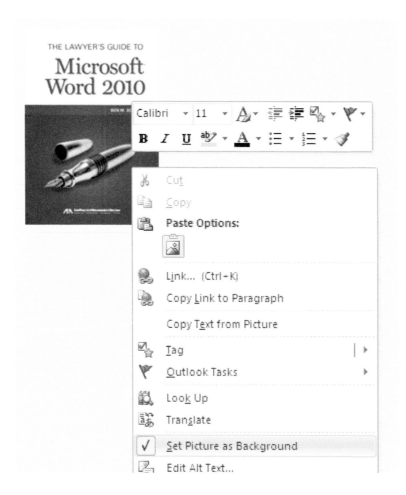

You might be tempted to use tables or graphical squares to create a calendar template. Resist that temptation. You'll discover that you're forced to choose between having a box you can type in which is easily moved or distorted, or having a box that stays put, which doesn't enforce its own borders (because it's a background image). Neither is a particularly good solution; either is likely to induce a fair bit of frustration.

Entire Sections

At Roland Schorr we have a shared notebook where we keep notes on all of our clients. Each client gets a section. Each client's section starts with 6 basic pages and we add additional pages as necessary. In order to make this process as easy as possible we created a blank, sample, section with the 6 basic pages inside it and we named it "NEW CLIENT TEMPLATE." When we need to create a section for a new client we right-click the NEW CLIENT TEMPLATE and choose **Copy** then copy it to the place in the notebook where we want it (see **Figure 57**). Once it's there, we rename that copy to the client's name and start populating it with the client's information.

Figure 57

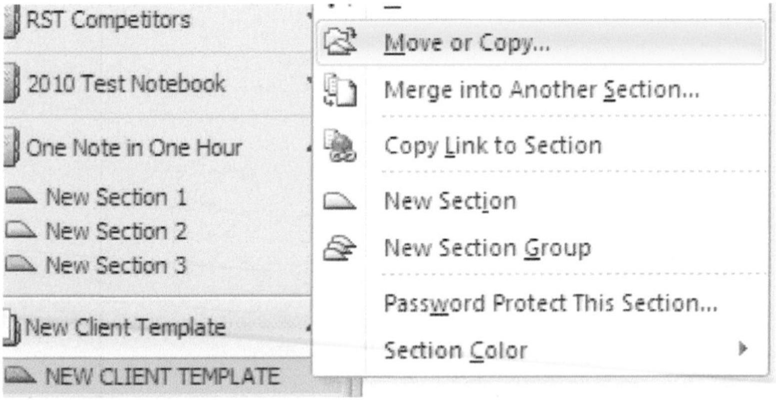

This technique saves us a lot of time in creating the new client section and ensures that we always have our 6 basic pages.

Searching Your Notes

Taking notes is useless unless you can find those notes later. Luckily OneNote provides us with a really powerful search capability to recover your notes later.

To search your notes just click in the search box at the top right corner of the notebook and type the word or phrase you're looking for (see **Figure 58**). You will have the option of limiting (or broadening) the scope of your search.

Figure 58

Stick the Search

When you run a search your search results open in a pane under the search bar (see **Figure 59**). If you're careful to just click on each result OneNote will display that page and leave the search results pane open. But . . . as soon as you click on the page with the result (to scroll up or down for example) your search results pane closes and to get it back you . . . have to re-run your search. Humbug!

Figure 59

However, there is a trick to give you an enduring search results pane. When you run your search, click the "Open Note and Audio Search results pane" link at the bottom of the search results pane (see **Figure 60**).

Figure 60

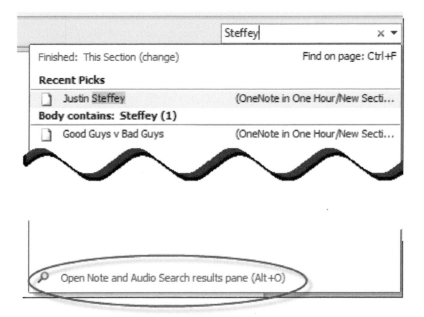

That will open a persistent box on the right side of the screen that lets you sift through the search results, and click on the actual pages, without that search results box closing.

Searching Images

One of the neat tricks OneNote has up its sleeve is that if you insert any pictures or images into your notes OneNote will scan the image for any readable text and will automatically OCR (Optical Character Recognition) that text so it's searchable. Take a photo of a shop sign and put it in your notes. Search for a word on that sign and OneNote will find (among other possible matches) the sign.

Naturally that depends upon the picture being good enough—and the sign being good enough—that OneNote can actually recognize the words, but I find that the success rate is very very high.

Searching Audio

OneNote will automatically search your audio as well as your text when you use the search box at the top right. If for some reason that doesn't seem to be working there are three possible reasons for that:

1. The word you're looking for doesn't actually exist in the recording.
2. The "Enable searching audio and video recordings for words" option isn't turned on. Go to File | Options | Audio & Video in OneNote and make sure the box for that is checked as it is in **Figure 61**.
3. The sound quality of the recording was too poor for OneNote to get an accurate transcription.

Figure 61

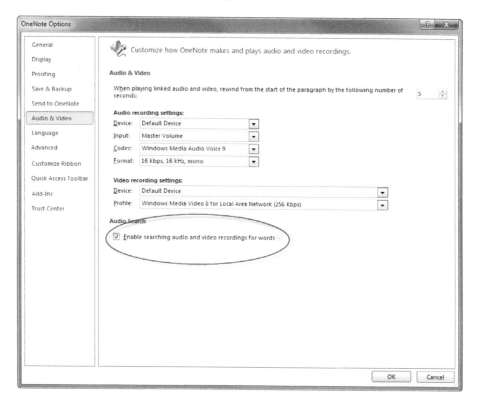

Having a higher quality microphone can help with #3 and is a good idea if you plan to do a lot of audio recording.

Changing the Scope

When you do your first search it will likely search all of your note-books at once. If you'd like to refine the scope of your search click the "Type to search in: All Notebooks (change)" link at the top of the search results box (see **Figure 62**) and choose what you'd like to limit it to. Your choices are This Section, This Section Group, This Note-book or All Notebooks.

Figure 62

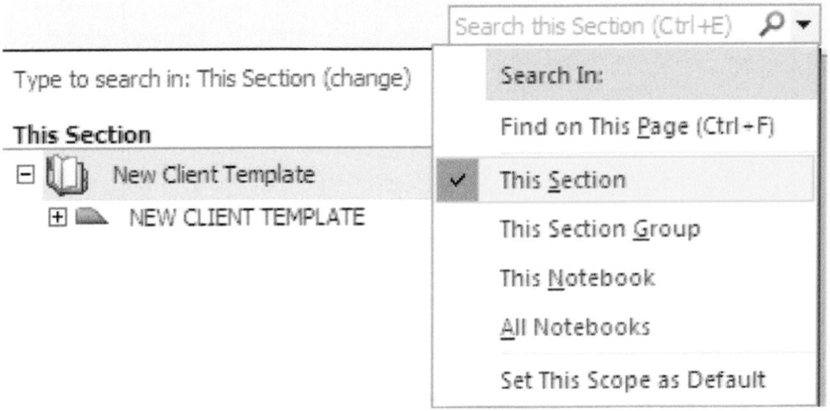

If you just want to search the current page, press **CTRL+F** instead of using the default search box.

Also, if you'd like the new scope to be the default scope after you do the search on that newly limited scope ("This section" for example) click the "Type to search in: . . . (change)" link again and this time instead of changing the scope click the "Set This Scope as Default" link at the bottom (you can see it on **Figure 62** above). From then on your searches will default to the new scope.

Searching for Tags

Applying tags is fine, but you're only getting a fraction of their usefulness if you don't use the "Find Tags" tool to work with them. On the Home tab of the Ribbon click **Find Tags** and you'll get the Tags Summary task pane that you see in **Figure 63**.

Figure 63

At the top you have a field that lets you choose how you want the tags grouped. The default is "Tag name" so that all of the tags of the same kind are grouped together regardless of what page they're on. It's also useful to group them by date so that you have the tags chronologically (by date applied) and, if you're searching across an entire notebook) grouping by section can be useful.

Next you have a checkbox that gives you the opportunity to exclude checked items. This is only going to apply to a subset of the tags—namely the checkboxes.

Below that you'll see the list of tagged items themselves. If you click on any of those items OneNote will take you to the place in your notes where that item is. It's a quick way to navigate through your items.

Towards the bottom of the Tags Summary task pane you'll find a selection box that lets you tell OneNote the scope you want to search. The current Page, Page Group (which means the current page and all subpages of the page), Section, Section Group, Notebook, All Notebooks or the subset of notes filtered by date. So you can tell it to show you all of the tags in the notes you've modified in the last week for example (see **Figure 64**).

Figure 64

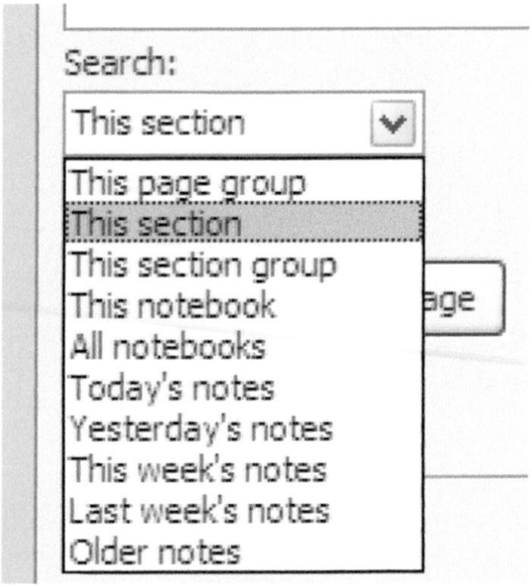

Search:

This section ▾

This page group
This section
This section group
This notebook
All notebooks
Today's notes
Yesterday's notes
This week's notes
Last week's notes
Older notes

Some users will just leave the Tags Summary pane open all the time and click the **Refresh Results** button to update it periodically. Others (like me) will just open it when we're going to use it, then close it again.

Finally the **Create Summary Page** button will create a page that is a list of all of the tags displayed in the Tags Summary (see **Figure 65**). Sort of like a static index page. Keep in mind that this summary page is a report; it's a copy of all of your tagged notes. Any changes you make to the summary page or the original notes will have nothing to do with the other.

Figure 65

Using OneNote for Research

In addition to taking notes, OneNote is especially good as a place to collect research.

Web Content

Adding web content to your notebooks is one of the strengths of OneNote and there are a few ways to do it. Perhaps the easiest is to simply use your mouse to select the web content you want (in your browser) and then drag and drop that content where you want it in OneNote. OneNote will paste in your content, attempt to preserve the original formatting and automatically build a hyperlink back to the original content. Just like you see in **Figure 66**.

Figure 66

OneNote 2010

Pasted from <http://office.microsoft.com/en-us/onenote/>

Another way to do it is to select the content in your web browser and choose "Send to OneNote" from the context menu that appears (see **Figure 67**). Unsurprisingly this only works in Internet Explorer, natively, though there have been some 3rd-party add-ins in the past that promised to add this functionality to Chrome or Firefox with varying degrees of success.

Figure 67

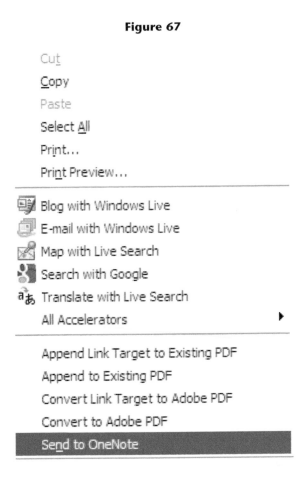

The other two ways you can do it include screen clippings (wait for it, we'll get there in a few pages) and printing to OneNote (that's coming too).

Documents and Files

OneNote has a couple of different ways to host documents and files. You can insert a link to a file stored on your hard drive or network; you can insert the content of the files or you can insert the file itself.

Inserting a link is a good choice because the file remains in your file system, people can still access the file without OneNote and it will always be current and in-sync. The downside is that you have to have access to the file you're linked to. So if you're linked to a file that is located on your network server but you're on an airplane over Illinois with no access to your server you won't be able to access that file.

Inserting the content of the document into OneNote as a printout lets you read it, annotate it and access it without having to open a third-party program. But if you insert the content it's harder to edit and work with. It may be searchable and you can read and annotate it but it's harder to send to a 3rd party and you lose all of the features of the originating program.

Finally you can just insert the file itself into OneNote. That gives you the portability of taking the document wherever your notebook goes and the flexibility to edit the document in its native application

To insert a file into OneNote—in any of those fashions—open Windows Explorer, find the file you want to insert, and drag/drop it into the OneNote page where you want to put it. You'll get the "Insert File Options dialog box that you see in **Figure 68**.

Figure 68

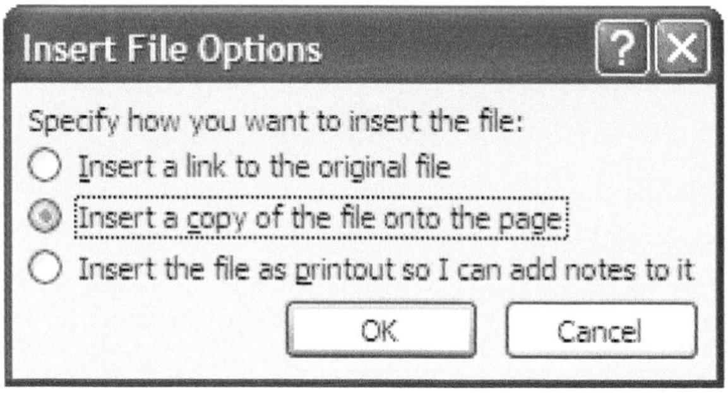

65

Images

You can insert images to OneNote by copying and pasting, dragging and dropping or going to the Insert tab of the Ribbon and clicking **Picture** 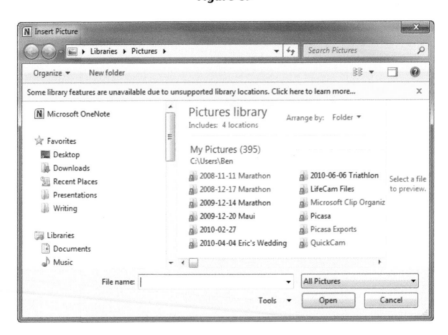. From there you can select an image from a file on your hard drive and insert it into OneNote (see **Figure 69**).

Figure 69

I frequently use this feature in a variety of ways. Such as. . . .

- If I'm at a meeting where they're using a whiteboard, I'll use my camera phone to take a picture of the whiteboard before it's erased and insert that picture into my notes.
- At a client's site I will often take a photo of key equipment and include those photos.

- Before taking apart something I may have to put back together I'll often take a photo of it and include that in my project notes. Then I have a record of what it looked like before.
- I've been known to photograph the client's business card and paste that into the notes about that client.

Print to OneNote

When you install Microsoft OneNote on a machine a new printer is added to the machines printers list called "Send to OneNote 2010" (see **Figure 70**). From any application that has the ability to print you can choose that printer as the destination for your print job and your data will be printed to OneNote. It'll look just like a paper printout and it will be completely searchable by OneNote.

Figure 70

One thing to be aware of, we've sometimes seen the behavior that when you install OneNote 2010 the installer creates the printer and then sets the printer to be the system default. If that happens to you, and assuming you don't want the OneNote Printer to be the default, go into your printer settings (Through Control Panel, generally) right click the printer you DO want to be you default and select Set as Default Printer. It should look very similar to what you see in **Figure 71**.

Figure 71

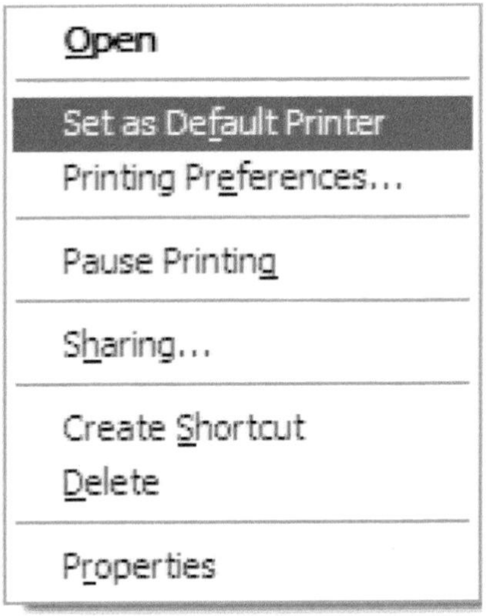

I've frequently used this tool to insert "printouts" of PDF files into OneNote. Those files become full text searchable and I can keep them with the rest of my notes.

Screen Clippings

One of the more interesting and unexpected features of OneNote is the ability to capture areas of your screen. If you press **Windows Key + S** the screen will go opaque and you can use your mouse to drag over an area of the screen (usually from one corner to the opposite corner; such as top left to bottom right). **Figure 72** shows what it looks like when you've selected a portion of the screen. When you let go of the left mouse button the area you selected will be copied to the clipboard and pasted onto a OneNote page.

Figure 72

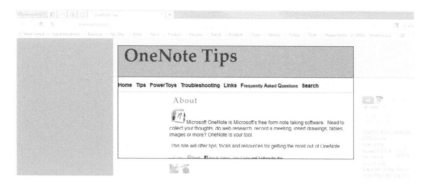

You can adjust where the screen clippings go in OneNote. I set mine to ONLY go to the clipboard, for example. From there I can paste the screen clipping wherever I want it. Onto a OneNote page or even into a Word Document or image editor if I like.

To edit where your screen clippings go to OneNote and click File | Options | Send to OneNote. The last option is "Screen clippings" and you can change it to "To Clipboard Only," "Always ask" or "Set default location" (see **Figure 73**).

One of my clients does quite a lot of real estate law and he will pull up Google Maps, find a satellite photo of the property in question, and use the OneNote screen clipping tool to cut the satellite image of the property to a page in OneNote. There he can use the drawing tools to illustrate and annotate the image.

Figure 73

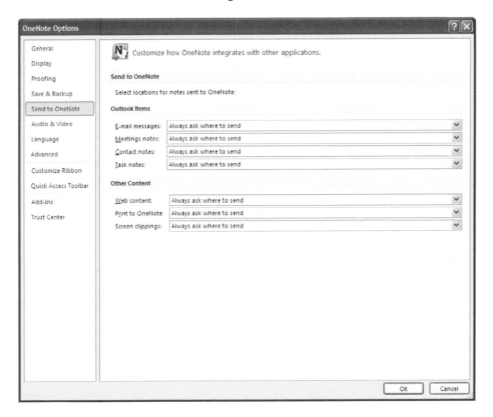

Sharing Notebooks

Taking notes is great. Sharing notes is better. You can share any notebook you want with other members of your team. (Note: All OneNote sharing happens at the notebook level. If you want to share an individual section you'll need to move that section into its own notebook)

Via Windows File Share

In our firm we have several OneNote notebooks located on our main file server. All of us can access those notebooks simply by going to File | Open and selecting the notebooks we want to open from the network drive (see **Figure 74**). Once you open a shared notebook in OneNote it

Figure 74

will get cached to the local hard drive—which means even when you're not connected to that shared location you can access the notes . . . or at least the notes as of the last time you were connected to that shared location. OneNote quietly synchronizes the notes in the background any time you are connected to the shared location.

The next time OneNote detects that you're connected to that shared location it will automatically synchronize any changes that have been made to the local version or the network version. If conflicting changes have been made to both then OneNote will prompt you as to how you want to handle that.

Via SkyDrive

If you have a Windows Live account (and they're free, so why not) you can store your OneNote 2010 notebooks on SkyDrive. As we talked about in Chapter 1 this is a handy way to share notebooks between machines that aren't on the same local network.

If you'd like to share a notebook you've already created on Sky-Drive first you have to make sure it's located in a Shared Folder.

OneNote Web App

Notebooks stored on SkyDrive can be opened in your browser simply by going to **http://office.live.com** and logging into your SkyDrive. Select your notebook and choose "Open in Browser" and you'll get the web app version of OneNote just like in **Figure 75**. It's a tad primitive, and it doesn't currently support ink (among other things) but for basic note taking and editing it's pretty good. And free.

If you have a OneNote notebook on SkyDrive that does NOT exist in your desktop OneNote (for example a notebook somebody else created and shared with you) you can add it to your desktop OneNote by clicking the **Open in OneNote** button you see on the right-end of the Ribbon in **Figure 75**.

Figure 75

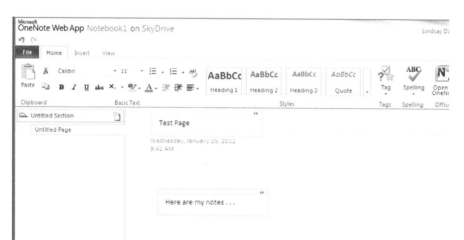

OneNote for iPhone

If you've got an iPhone then you'll really want to make use of Sky-Drive because you can download OneNote for iOS from the Apple App Store and install it on your iPhone. As of this writing it's still free and available in most English-speaking countries. Once it's installed you log into your **Live.com** account and it will synchronize your notebooks from SkyDrive to the iPhone.

Does it work on the iPad? Well . . . sort of. Yes, it will run on the iPad but it doesn't scale very well to the bigger screen. So it works . . . but it doesn't look very good. While there hasn't (as of this writing) been an official announcement of an iPad version of the app, the rumors are that one will be released some time in 2012.

The iPhone app doesn't support ink or tables yet.

Via SharePoint

You can host your OneNote notebooks in SharePoint if you have a SharePoint site. To move a notebook from your local hard drive to SharePoint, close the notebook in OneNote by right-clicking the notebook and selecting close (see **Figure 76**). Then go to the SharePoint document library where you want to host the OneNote notebook and upload the notebook from your hard drive to the library.

Figure 76

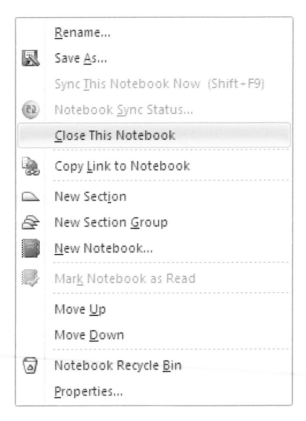

That done, click on the notebook in SharePoint and select "Open with OneNote." OneNote will open the notebook and begin syncing it to the local cache file. It'll look just the way it did when it was stored locally except that it will have the icon indicating it's synchronization status   since it now HAS a synchronization status.

In addition to our network file share we also share quite a few of our notebooks via the SharePoint Online module of Microsoft's Office

365. It's pretty slick and means that the notebooks we share that way automatically synchronize any time we have an Internet connection.

Via E-mail

If you'd like to share your notes via e-mail OneNote makes that pretty easy. Simply go to the page you want to share and click the **E-mail Page** button on the Home tab of the Ribbon [icon]. OneNote will create an e-mail message for you with your note content in the body of the HTML message like the one you can see in **Figure 77**. The other per-

Figure 77

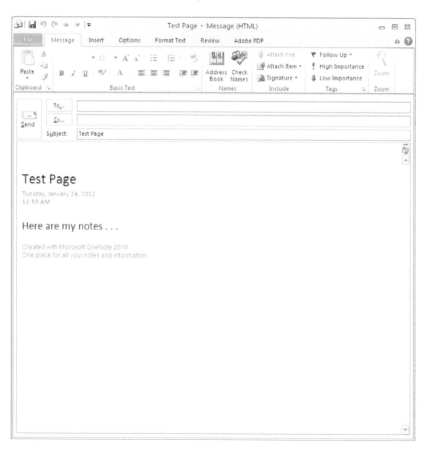

son doesn't even have to have OneNote to see your notes, though OneNote will also attach a .ONE file containing the page to the message so if the other person DOES have OneNote they can open (and save) it themselves.

I used to delete the .ONE file since I rarely find myself sharing notes via e-mail with people who have OneNote. The HTML representation of my notes is just fine. I said "used to" above because there's a setting in OneNote that lets you disable creating the .ONE attachment when you e-mail your notes. I'll explain how in Appendix A.

Permissions and Security

OneNote tends to take a fairly casual approach to security in most cases. There isn't a way to mark an individual page as secure or even read-only. You can encrypt an entire section (see below) to give it a password but be forewarned there are a number of 3rd party products available on the Internet that claim to be able to break OneNote passwords. I haven't tested any of them, but just fair warning—I wouldn't rely only on OneNote passwords for extremely confidential information.

You do, however, have other options. Since OneNote sections are .ONE files and notebooks are represented as a folder structure you CAN use regular Windows security to lock them down somewhat. For example if you want to make a section read-only you can set the read-only attribute on the .ONE file (see **Figure 78**) and you can even specify which user accounts have read-only vs. edit access if you have user accounts set up in your file share (see **Figure 79**).

We're teetering on the edge of a big rabbit hole when we start talking about Windows security so I'll leave it there. Just know that if you want granular security on your OneNote notebooks that OneNote provides very few options itself but you can use some of the Windows file/folder security features to enforce those things.

Figure 78

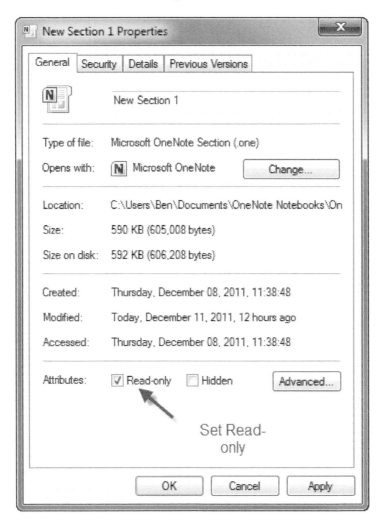

Last Modified/by

One thing OneNote does provide on shared notebooks is an indication of who the last person to modify a note was and when that happened. As you can see in **Figure 80** notes get tagged with a little colored bar and the initials of the last user to modify that particular note. If you

Figure 79

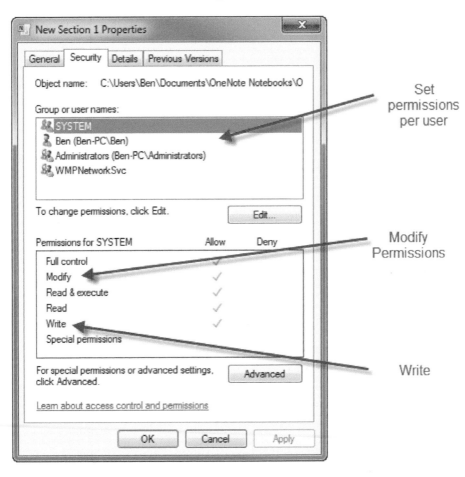

Set
permissions
per user

Modify
Permissions

Write

Figure 80

hover your mouse cursor over the initials you'll see the user's full name and the date and time the note was modified (see **Figure 81**).

If you don't see any author information there are two likely reasons.

Figure 81

1. On the View tab of the Ribbon make sure "Hide Authors" isn't enabled (see **Figure 82**).

Figure 82

2. The notebook might not be shared. OneNote doesn't bother to display the author tags on a notebook with only one author. You can still see the last modified information though if you point your mouse at the note container handle (the little square with the four-headed arrow that appears to the left of the note container) and right-click you'll see the last modified info at the bottom of the context menu (see **Figure 83**).

Figure 83

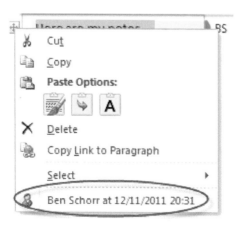

Encrypted Sections

If you have any sensitive data in OneNote you may want to password protect that section in order to encrypt it. To password protect a section just right-click the section either on the tabs or on the navigation pane and choose "Password Protect This Section" (see **Figure 84**).

Figure 84

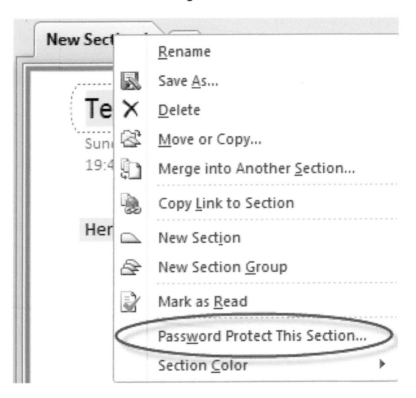

The Password Protection task pane will open as you can see in **Figure 85**. Click **Set Password** and you'll be prompted to enter your desired password (twice) and click **OK**. From that point on you'll need to enter the password whenever you try to open that section. Be sure to select a good password—length is more important than complexity. I recommend that you use a phrase rather than a word.

Figure 85

"How 'bout them Yankees!" is actually a pretty good passphrase. Long, not hard to remember, not too hard to type, mixed case with letters and symbols.

"My 2 dogs are cute" isn't bad either. Pick a phrase you can remember but that isn't easy to guess. Ideally something at least 12 characters long (and yes, the spaces count). Song lyrics are often a good choice.

NOTE: if you haven't unlocked the section with the password any searches you do on that notebook will NOT include content from that section. If you want to search the entire notebook, including password protected sections, you'll need to go to the password protected section(s) and unlock them with the password.

The other important thing to know about password protected sections is something I said earlier in this book—they're good but not ironclad. If you're protecting highly sensitive data you may want to use OneNote password protection as just one layer of your security—not as the whole onion.

Working with Other Apps

OneNote 2010 comes with every version of Office 2010 and as you might suspect includes very good integration with the other Office apps.

Outlook

Outlook is the application that integrates the most tightly with OneNote. In Outlook 2010 you'll find **OneNote** buttons scattered throughout  to do things like send e-mail, contacts or calendar items to OneNote.

E-mails

You can send e-mails from Outlook to OneNote by clicking the **OneNote** button on the home tab of Outlook's Ribbon (see **Figure 86**). A dialog

Figure 86

box will appear that asks what section (and even what page if you like) to send the message to (see **Figure 87**). If you don't select a specific page then OneNote will create a new page and put the e-mail there.

Figure 87

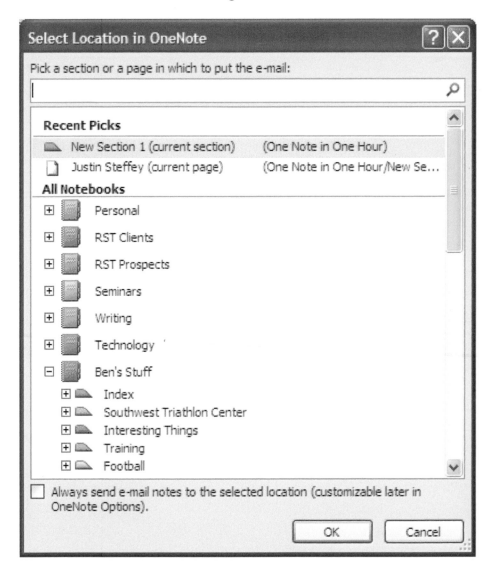

What you'll get is a page that looks like **Figure 88**. In a little table at the top you have the basic info about the message (including a clickable MailTo: link) and below that the full text of the message which can be annotated, searched and shared.

Figure 88

Avoid the temptation to use OneNote as a massive archive of e-mail. It's not really well-suited to that kind of data collection. It's better for storing/collecting selected messages about a project or matter.

Contacts

When you click the **Linked Contact Notes** button in Outlook you'll create a page in OneNote that has that contact's information on it like the one you see in **Figure 89**. OneNote will also automatically build a link back to the Outlook item so that you can easily return to the source.

Figure 89

Schorr, Ben

Wednesday, January 25, 2012
10:23 AM

Contact	Schorr, Ben Roland Schorr & Tower
Business Phone	(928) 377-5630
Business Address	4701 E. La Quinta Way Flagstaff, AZ 86004
E-mail	bens@rolandschorr.com
Home Phone	(808) 782-6306

Link to Outlook item

Notes

I sometimes use this feature to create a page in OneNote with my primary contact(s) information that goes in the section with the rest of the client/matter information. The page is a good place for keeping various random notes about the contact.

Appointments

A great way to take notes in a meeting—click the **Linked Appointment Notes** button in your Outlook appointment item and create a OneNote page for the meeting (see **Figure 90**).

On that page you can write any notes you want, flag action items, even scribble with the ink/drawing features we talked about in **Lesson 2**.

Figure 90

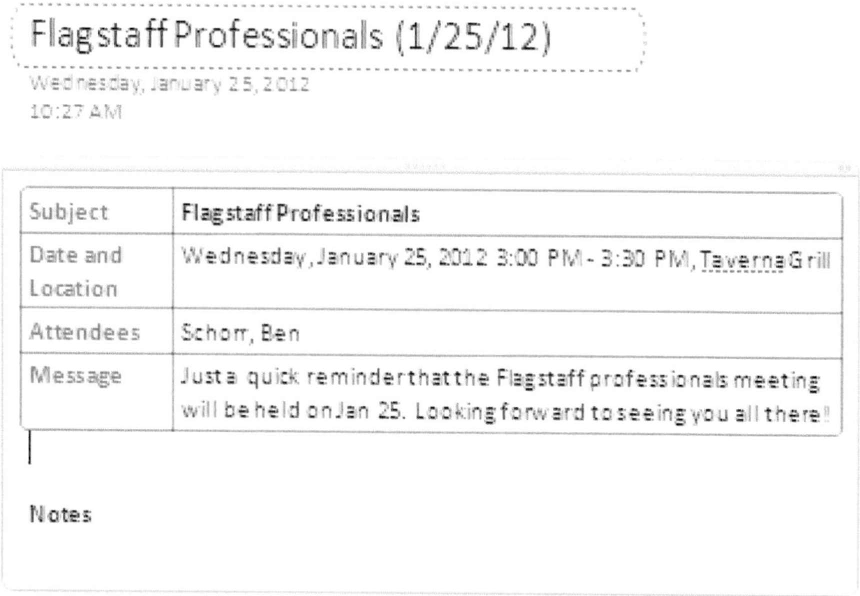

Flagstaff Professionals (1/25/12)

Wednesday, January 25, 2012
10:27 AM

Subject	Flagstaff Professionals
Date and Location	Wednesday, January 25, 2012 3:00 PM – 3:30 PM, Taverna Grill
Attendees	Schorr, Ben
Message	Just a quick reminder that the Flagstaff professionals meeting will be held on Jan 25. Looking forward to seeing you all there!

Notes

Flagged Tasks

OneNote and Outlook support bi-directional synchronization of tasks. That means you can create a task in OneNote, flag it for Outlook and have it appear on your Outlook To Do Bar. Check it complete in either product and it will be marked as complete in both places.

To flag a task in OneNote for inclusion on your Outlook task list click on the note item to select it then click the **Outlook Tasks** button on the OneNote Ribbon and select the follow-up date you want (see **Figure 91**). OneNote will place a flag in front of the task that looks just like the For Follow Up flags in Outlook; as you can see in **Figure 92**— simple as that.

More importantly your task will now ALSO appear on the Outlook To-Do Bar (see **Figure 93**).

Figure 91

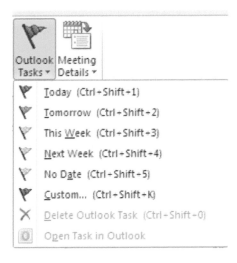

Figure 92

Figure 93

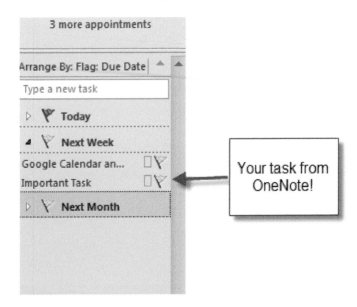

To mark the item as complete just left click on the flag in either Outlook or OneNote—it'll be marked as complete in both as soon as the synchronization completes (see **Figure 94**). This can take a minute or so sometimes; be patient.

Figure 94

✔ Important Task

Word

Integration between OneNote and Word is a little less formal than the integration between OneNote and Outlook but there is still a nice synergy.

Starting a Document

I'll frequently start a long Word document in OneNote by creating an outline. "You can create an outline in Word!" you're probably thinking. Yes, that's true, but in OneNote I can create an outline and annotate that outline with research items from other documents, e-mails and the web to give me ideas and content for fleshing out my content. Once I have a fairly robust outline I'll send that content to Word by clicking File | Send | Send to Word (see **Figure 95**).

Linked Notes

If you're working on a document and want to take notes that are related to the document OneNote 2010 lets you create linked notes. Linked notes are notes that are associated with the page in question in Word.

The way it works is that you put OneNote in docked view by pressing **CTRL+ALT+D** or clicking the **Dock to Desktop** button  so that you get a view that looks like **Figure 96**. As you work on the doc-

Figure 95

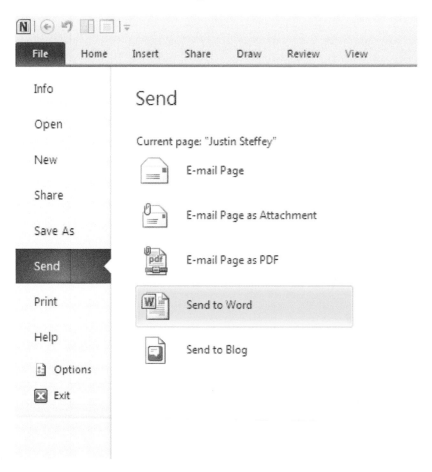

ument and take notes—presumably switching back and forth between Word and OneNote as you go—OneNote remembers which page you were on in the Word document when you took a particular note. Then, later, when reviewing those notes, you'll be able to click the linked note hyperlink to take you right back to that part of the Word document (see **Figure 97**).

Your notes are associated with your text. Nifty.

Figure 96

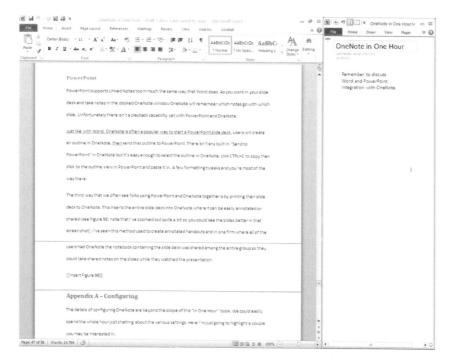

Figure 97

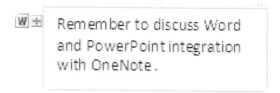

PowerPoint

PowerPoint supports Linked Notes too in much the same way that
Word does. As you work in your slide deck and take notes in the
docked OneNote window OneNote will remember which notes go
with which slide. Unfortunately there isn't a playback capability yet
with PowerPoint and OneNote.

Just like with Word, OneNote is often a popular way to start a PowerPoint slide deck. Users will create an outline in OneNote, then send that outline to PowerPoint. There isn't any built in "Send to PowerPoint" in OneNote but it's easy enough to select the outline in OneNote, click **CTRL+C** to copy then click to the outline view in PowerPoint and paste it in. A few formatting tweaks and you're most of the way there.

The third way that we often see folks using PowerPoint and OneNote together is by printing their slide deck to OneNote. This inserts the entire slide deck into OneNote where it can be easily annotated or shared (see **Figure 98**; note that I've zoomed out quite a bit so you could see the slides better in that screen shot). I've seen this method used to create annotated handouts and in one firm where all of the users had OneNote the notebook containing the slide deck was shared among the entire group so they could take shared notes on the slides while they watched the presentation.

Figure 98

Configuring

The details of configuring OneNote are beyond the scope of this "In One Hour" book. We could easily spend the whole hour just chatting about the various settings. Here I'm just going to highlight a couple you may be interested in.

Backups

OneNote will automatically create backups of its notebooks on a regular basis. Two settings you may want to configure are WHERE the backups get created and how often.

The where is actually the bigger of the two questions. Ideally it should be on an external drive or network location, not the same drive that the notebooks or cache file live on normally. That way when your local hard drive dies, it doesn't take your notebooks AND the backups with it.

To configure your backups go to File | Options | Save and Backup as you can see in **Figure 99**. In the first section you can see where you can click "Backup Folder" and then the **Modify** button to choose where you would like your OneNote backups stored.

If you have a network server location you can use that would be perfect. If not, perhaps an external hard drive connected to your computer via USB?

In the backup section of that screen you can enable (or disable) automatic backups and specify how often they should occur. As you

Figure 99

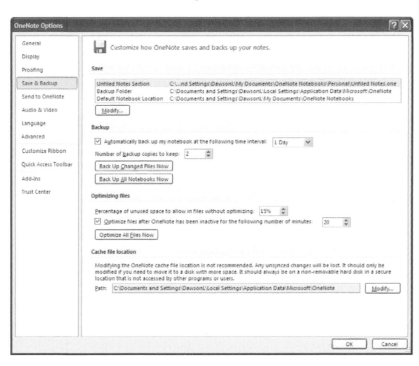

can see in **Figure 100** you can specify intervals ranging from minutes to weeks. I usually recommend 1 day.

If you want to initiate an immediate backup of your notes you can click the **Back Up Changed Files Now** or **Back Up All Notebooks Now** button.

To restore from Backup you have to go to the backups location and open the backed up notebook from there. You can then copy any pages/ sections (or the entire notebook) from that location back to your production notebook. One catch . . . the actual backup files are stored in a subfolder of the folder you specified. For example: my backups are set to go to T:\OneNote (as you can see in Figure 99 above). But when you get there you discover that the actual backed up notebooks are in T:\OneNote\14.0\Backup.

Figure 100

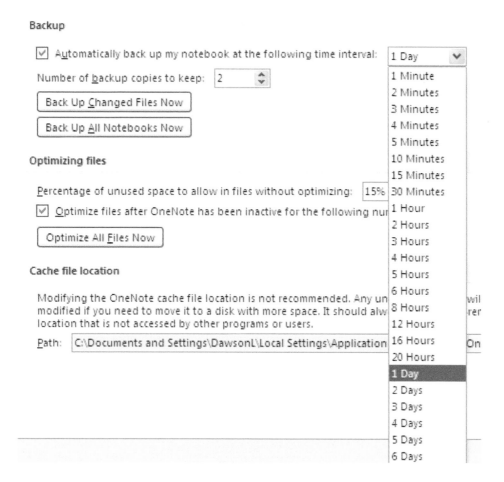

Personalize

On the File | Options menu under the General group you'll find the Personalize settings (see **Figure 101**). These settings are pretty self-explanatory but they're also pretty important if you're going to do any collaboration. Here's where you specify your username and initials that OneNote (and, in fact, the rest of the Office suite) will use to identify your notes, comments and contributions.

Figure 101

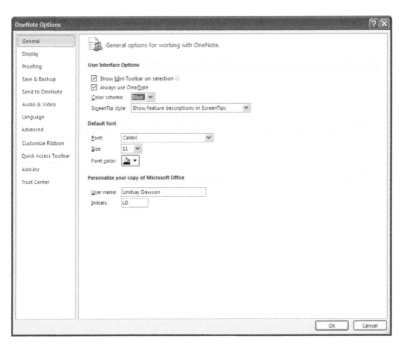

Advanced

One thing I want to point out on the Advanced tab of File | Options is featured in **Figure 102**. It's the settings that control how OneNote will e-mail your notes if you ask it to by clicking the **E-mail** button . Especially notice the setting that lets you disable attaching a copy of your notes as a OneNote file. I usually disable that—the attachment it creates is useless to anybody who doesn't have OneNote.

Figure 102

Troubleshooting

When things go wrong with OneNote, and they occasionally do, there are a few steps you can take to troubleshoot.

Safe Mode

One quick troubleshooting step you can take with OneNote is to start it with the /safeboot switch. Start | Run | Onenote /safeboot (see **Figure 103**). OneNote will start and present you with a couple of trouble-shooting options (see **Figure 104**). One of these options is to clear the OneNote cache (see **Figure 104**) and the other is to clear the customized user settings, which basically resets OneNote back to the default.

Figure 103

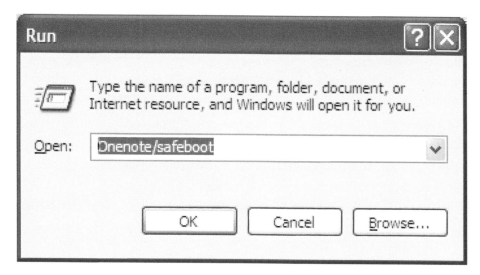

Figure 104

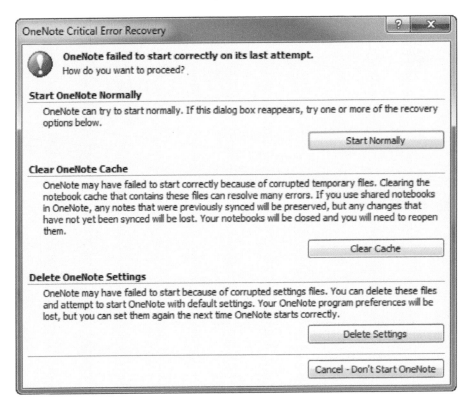

Rename the Cache

Sometimes the cache file can get corrupted and renaming it can help to resolve the issue.

OneNote uses a local cache file to improve performance, reliability and sharing. All work in OneNote is actually done to the local cache file rather than the actual data file and then those changes are quietly sync'd to the data file in the background.

Sometimes the cache in OneNote 2007 or 2010 can get corrupted and the best way to troubleshoot it is to delete it. Assuming all of the changes you have made have already been committed to the data file deleting the cache will not lose any data—but if you're at the point where you're deleting the cache file you're probably fairly desperate anyhow so a little bit of data loss may be an acceptable price to pay to get the application back on its feet.

The cache file for OneNote 2007 is typically found in the: C:\Users\ [username]\AppData\Local\Microsoft\OneNote\12.0 folder if you're running Vista or Windows 7 or the C:\Documents and Settings\[user name]\application data\local\Microsoft\OneNote\12.0 folder for Windows XP. For OneNote 2010 just change the "12" to a "14."

With OneNote closed, using Windows Explorer go to that folder, find the OneNoteOfflineCache.onecache file and either rename it, move it or delete it. I usually recommend renaming it so that if this fix doesn't work you can always rename it back.

Again, if you have changes in the cache file that have NOT been committed to the primary file you'll lose them if you delete the cache file. Usually best to rename it to something else like "OneNoteOffline Cache.oldcache." If letting OneNote create the new cache solves the problem and you haven't lost any important data then you can always just delete the .oldcache file later.

When you start OneNote it will automatically recreate the cache file; hopefully without whatever corruption caused the problem.

The Recycle Bin

OneNote 2007 removed the Recycle Bin feature that OneNote 2003 had for undeleting notes. Why? Because usage statistics showed that almost nobody ever used it. But users clamored to have it back and the OneNote team began to suspect that maybe nobody used it because they didn't know how.

So the Recycle Bin is back in OneNote 2010 and a bit easier to use. If you go to the Share tab of the Ribbon you'll see the **Notebook Recycle Bin** button . Click the button and you'll see a "section" that is comprised entirely of pages you've deleted like the one in **Figure 105**. If you've also deleted any sections you'll see those listed as section tabs in the Recycle Bin.

Figure 105

To undelete a page or section from the Recycle Bin you need to right-click it and choose "Move or Copy" to move it back to where you want it to be.

Worth noting—the Recycle Bin only helps you recover deleted pages and sections. It won't help you recover an individual note container that you deleted. If that happened the best thing to do is to immediately press **CTRL+Z** (Undo).

If you can't Undo your deletion then the next best thing you can do to recover a delete note item is go to a previous version of the page.

1. Go to the Share tab of the Ribbon.
2. Click the **Page Versions** button (see **Figure 106**).
3. On the pages list you should now see one or more older versions of that page. Their tabs will be gray and will list the data and user who last modified that page (see **Figure 107**).

Figure 106

Figure 107

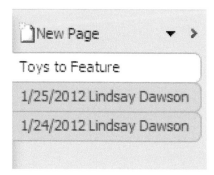

4. Look at the most recent of those older versions and see if the note you need is there. If so, copy and paste it back into your current note. If not keep looking through successively older versions of the page until you find it.

If you don't find it, or if there aren't any older versions . . . then you'll have to go to OneNote's backups and see if it's there. To do that you need to click File | Open, navigate to your OneNote backup location (we talked about it in **Appendix A**) and open the backed up version of the section. See if you can find your old note item there and copy/paste it to the current version.

If that doesn't work . . . well, you can try going to your regular file backups. Presumably you're backing your data up to an external hard drive, network server, tape, Internet backup service (like Mozy or Carbonite).

If that doesn't work . . . then you're probably out of luck. You'll just have to do your best to recreate the note from memory I suppose. Fortunately the most likely scenario where NONE of those things would work is a note that you created very recently—so recently none of your backups had time to capture the note. So you're more likely to be able to recreate it if you have to.

More Resources

The Internet is like a river . . . you step in but the water has moved on. The sites and URLs I'm going to provide in this lesson are working fine as of this writing, but I can't guarantee they'll still be there as of this reading. If you get an error, give Google a chance to find the site for you. Maybe it just moved downstream somewhere.

OneNote-Tips (http://www.onenote-tips.com)

A site with tips and tricks for working with OneNote. It's updated fairly regularly and covers all versions of the product.

OfficeForLawyers (http://www.officeforlawyers.com)

Not specifically a OneNote site it has information on the entire Microsoft Office suite (including OneNote) as well as general technology advice aimed at attorneys.

Microsoft (http://www.microsoft.com/onenote)

The mother ship. Microsoft's official OneNote site includes articles, videos, templates and other content specifically for OneNote.

OneNote Team Blogs

- Daniel Escapa—One of the lead product managers on OneNote and a very knowledgeable fellow Daniel has a really good blog on OneNote that you can find here: **http://blogs.msdn.com/b/descapa/**
- John Guin—John is the lead test engineer on OneNote and his blog, which is sometimes a bit more technical and sometimes a bit more whimsical than Daniels, is also an excellent source of information. You can find it here: **http://blogs.msdn.com/b/johnguin/**

Forums

If you have a OneNote question you need answered, consider visiting Microsoft's Answers forums—staffed by MVPs (and occasionally by the OneNote team themselves) it's a great place to ask questions and get answers from your peers. There are even thousands of questions there that have already been asked (and answered) you may well find your question is one of them.

You can find the Microsoft Answers forum for OneNote here: **http://answers.microsoft.com/en-us/office/forum/onenote**

Index

SELECTED BOOKS FROM

Law Practice Management Section
MARKETING • MANAGEMENT • TECHNOLOGY • FINANCE

The Lawyer's Guide to Collaboration Tools and Technologies: Smart Ways to Work Together
By Dennis Kennedy and Tom Mighell

Product Code: 5110589 / LPM Price: $59.95 / Regular Price: $89.95

This first-of-its-kind guide for the legal profession shows you how to use standard technology you already have and the latest "Web 2.0" resources and other tech tools, like Google Docs, Microsoft Office and Share-Point, and Adobe Acrobat, to work more effectively on projects with colleagues, clients, co-counsel and even opposing counsel. In *The Lawyer's Guide to Collaboration Tools and Technologies: Smart Ways to Work Together*, well-known legal technology authorities Dennis Kennedy and Tom Mighell provides a wealth of information useful to lawyers who are just beginning to try these tools, as well as tips and techniques for those lawyers with intermediate and advanced collaboration experience.

Google for Lawyers: Essential Search Tips and Productivity Tools
By Carole A. Levitt and Mark E. Rosch

Product Code: 5110704 / LPM Price: $47.95 / Regular Price: $79.95

This book introduces novice Internet searchers to the diverse collection of information locatable through Google. The book discusses the importance of including effective Google searching as part of a lawyer's due diligence, and cites case law that mandates that lawyers should use Google and other resources available on the Internet, where applicable. For intermediate and advanced users, the book unlocks the power of various advanced search strategies and hidden search features they might not be aware of.

The Lawyer's Guide to Adobe Acrobat, Third Edition
By David L. Masters

Product Code: 5110588 / LPM Price: $49.95 / Regular Price: $79.95

This book was written to help lawyers increase productivity, decrease costs, and improve client services by moving from paper-based files to digital records. This updated and revised edition focuses on the ways lawyers can benefit from using the most current software, Adobe® Acrobat 8, to create Portable Document Format (PDF) files.

PDF files are reliable, easy-to-use, electronic files for sharing, reviewing, filing, and archiving documents across diverse applications, business processes, and platforms. The format is so reliable that the federal courts' Case Management/Electronic Case Files (CM/ECF) program and state courts that use Lexis-Nexis File & Serve have settled on PDF as the standard.

You'll learn how to:

- Create PDF files from a number of programs, including Microsoft Office
- Use PDF files the smart way
- Markup text and add comments
- Digitally, and securely, sign documents
- Extract content from PDF files
- Create electronic briefs and forms

The Electronic Evidence and Discovery Handbook: Forms, Checklists, and Guidelines
By Sharon D. Nelson, Bruce A. Olson, and John W. Simek

Product Code: 5110569 / LPM Price: $99.95 / Regular Price: $129.95

The use of electronic evidence has increased dramatically over the past few years, but many lawyers still struggle with the complexities of electronic discovery. This substantial book provides lawyers with the templates they need to frame their discovery requests and provides helpful advice on what they can subpoena. In addition to the ready-made forms, the authors also supply explanations to bring you up to speed on the electronic discovery field. The accompanying CD-ROM features over 70 forms, including, Motions for Protective Orders, Preservation and Spoliation Documents, Motions to Compel, Electronic Evidence Protocol Agreements, Requests for Production, Internet Services Agreements, and more. Also included is a full electronic evidence case digest with over 300 cases detailed!

The Lawyer's Guide to Microsoft Word 2010
By Ben M. Schorr

Product Code: 5110721 / LPM Price: $41.95 / Regular Price: $69.95

Microsoft® Word is one of the most used applications in the Microsoft® Office suite. This handy reference includes clear explanations, legal-specific descriptions, and time-saving tips for getting the most out of Microsoft Word®—and customizing it for the needs of today's legal professional. Focusing on the tools and features that are essential for lawyers in their everyday practice, this book explains in detail the key components to help make you more effective, more efficient, and more successful.

The Lawyer's Guide to LexisNexis CaseMap
By Daniel J. Siegel

Product Code: 5110715 / LPM Price: $47.95 / Regular Price: $79.95

LexisNexis CaseMap is a computer program that makes analyzing cases easier and allows lawyers to do a better job for their clients in less time. Many consider this an essential law office tool. If you are interested in learning more about LexisNexis CaseMap, this book will help you:

- Analyze the strengths and weaknesses of your cases quickly and easily;
- Learn how to create files for people, organizations and issues, while avoiding duplication;
- Customize CaseMap so that you can get the most out of your data;
- Enter data so that you can easily prepare for trial, hearings, depositions, and motions for summary judgment;
- Import data from a wide range of programs, including Microsoft Outlook;
- Understand CaseMap's many Reports and ReportBooks;
- Use the Adobe DocPreviewer to import PDFs and quickly create facts and objects; and
- Learn how to perform advanced searches plus how to save and update your results.

Virtual Law Practice:
How to Deliver Legal Services Online
By Stephanie L. Kimbro

Product Code: 5110707 / LPM Price: $47.95 / Regular Price: $79.95

The legal market has recently experienced a dramatic shift as lawyers seek out alternative methods of practicing law and providing more affordable legal services. Virtual law practice is revolutionizing the way the public receives legal services and how legal professionals work with clients. If you are interested in this form of practicing law, *Virtual Law Practice* will help you:

- *Responsibly deliver legal services online to* your clients
- Successfully set up and operate a virtual law office
- Establish a virtual law practice online through a secure, client-specific portal
- Manage and market your virtual law practice
- Understand state ethics and advisory opinions
- Find more flexibility and work/life balance in the legal profession

The Lawyer's Essential Guide to Writing
By Marie Buckley

Product Code: 5110726 / LPM Price: $47.95 / Regular Price: $79.95

This is a readable, concrete guide to contemporary legal writing. Based on Marie Buckley's years of experience coaching lawyers, this book provides a systematic approach to all forms of written communication, from memoranda and briefs to e-mail and blogs. The book sets forth three principles for powerful writing and shows how to apply those principles to develop a clean and confident style.

iPad in One Hour for Lawyers
By Tom Mighell

Product Code: 5110719 / LPM Price: $19.95 / Regular Price: $34.95

Whether you are a new or a more advanced iPad user, *iPad in One Hour for Lawyers* takes a great deal of the mystery and confusion out of using your iPad. Ideal for lawyers who want to get up to speed swiftly, this book presents the essentials so you don't get bogged down in technical jargon and extraneous features and apps. In just six, short lessons, you'll learn how to:

- Quickly Navigate and Use the iPad User Interface
- Set Up Mail, Calendar, and Contacts
- Create and Use Folders to Multitask and Manage Apps
- Add Files to Your iPad, and Sync Them
- View and Manage Pleadings, Case Law, Contracts, and other Legal Documents
- Use Your iPad to Take Notes and Create Documents
- Use Legal-Specific Apps at Trial or in Doing Research

Find Info Like a Pro, Volume 1: Mining the Internet's Publicly Available Resources for Investigative Research
By Carole A. Levitt and Mark E. Rosch

Product Code: 5110708 / LPM Price: $47.95 / Regular Price: $79.95

This complete hands-on guide shares the secrets, shortcuts, and realities of conducting investigative and background research using the sources of publicly available information available on the Internet. Written for legal professionals, this comprehensive desk book lists, categorizes, and describes hundreds of free and fee-based Internet sites. The resources and techniques in this book are useful for investigations; depositions; locating missing witnesses, clients, or heirs; and trial preparation, among other research challenges facing legal professionals. In addition, a CD-ROM is included, which features clickable links to all of the sites contained in the book.

How to Start and Build a Law Practice, Platinum Fifth Edition
By Jay G Foonberg

Product Code: 5110508 / LPM Price: $57.95 / Regular Price: $69.95

This classic ABA bestseller has been used by tens of thousands of lawyers as the comprehensive guide to planning, launching, and growing a successful practice. It's packed with over 600 pages of guidance on identifying the right location, finding clients, setting fees, managing your office, maintaining an ethical and responsible practice, maximizing available resources, upholding your standards, and much more. You'll find the information you need to successfully launch your practice, run it at maximum efficiency, and avoid potential pitfalls along the way. If you're committed to starting—and growing—your own practice, this one book will give you the expert advice you need to make it succeed for years to come.

Social Media for Lawyers: The Next Frontier
By Carolyn Elefant and Nicole Black

Product Code: 5110710 / LPM Price: $47.95 / Regular Price: $79.95

The world of legal marketing has changed with the rise of social media sites such as Linkedin, Twitter, and Facebook. Law firms are seeking their companies attention with tweets, videos, blog posts, pictures, and online content. Social media is fast and delivers news at record pace. This book provides you with a practical, goal-centric approach to using social media in your law practice that will enable you to identify social media platforms and tools that fit your practice and implement them easily, efficiently, and ethically.

30-DAY RISK-FREE ORDER FORM

LawPracticeManagementSection
MARKETING • MANAGEMENT • TECHNOLOGY • FINANCE

Please print or type. To ship UPS, we must have your street address.
If you list a P.O. Box, we will ship by U.S. Mail.

Name _____

Member ID _____

Firm/Organization _____

Street Address _____

City/State/Zip _____

Area Code/Phone (In case we have a question about your order) _____

E-mail _____

Method of Payment:
❑ Check enclosed, payable to American Bar Association
❑ MasterCard   ❑ Visa   ❑ American Express

Card Number _____ Expiration Date _____

Signature Required _____

MAIL THIS FORM TO:
American Bar Association, Publication Orders
P.O. Box 10892, Chicago, IL 60610

ORDER BY PHONE:
24 hours a day, 7 days a week:
Call 1-800-285-2221 to place a credit card order.
We accept Visa, MasterCard, and American Express.

EMAIL ORDERS: orders@americanbar.org
FAX: 1-312-988-5568

VISIT OUR WEB SITE: www.ShopABA.org
Allow 7-10 days for regular UPS delivery. Need it
sooner? Ask about our overnight delivery options.
Call the ABA Service Center at 1-800-285-2221
for more information.

GUARANTEE:
If–for any reason–you are not satisfied with your
purchase, you may return it within 30 days of receipt for
a refund of the price of the book(s). No questions asked.

Thank You For Your Order.

Join the ABA Law Practice Management Section today and receive a substantial discount on Section publications!

Product Code:	Description:	Quantity:	Price:	Total Price:
				$
				$
				$
				$
				$
			Subtotal:	$
			*Tax:	$
			**Shipping/Handling:	$
			Yes, I am an ABA member and would like to join the Law Practice Management Section today! (Add $50.00)	$
			Total:	$

**Shipping/Handling:

$0.00 to $9.99	add $0.00
$10.00 to $49.99	add $5.95
$50.00 to $99.99	add $7.95
$100.00 to $199.99	add $9.95
$200.00 to $499.99	add $12.95

*Tax:
IL residents add 9.5%
DC residents add 6%